Arirang of Korea
Han, Sorrows and Hope

Arirang of Korea
Han, Sorrows and Hope

Copyright @ 2013 by Lee Chung-myun

First Published January 15th, 2013

Author Lee Chung-myun
Publisher Suh Yong-soon
Company Easy Publishing Co.

Address Room 903, World Officetel, 65-1, Unni-dong, Jongno-gu,
Seoul, Korea 110-350
Tel 82-2-743-7661, 82-2-743-7668
Fax 82-2-743-7621
E-mail easy7661@naver.com

The National Library of Korea Cataloging-in-Publication(CIP)
Includes bibliographical references and index
ISBN 978-89-92822-95-4 03900 : 38,000(US$ 40.00)
679.311-KDC5
781.62957-DDC21   CIP 2013000103

Printed in Korea

Arirang of Korea
Han, Sorrows and Hope

Lee Chung-myun

Professor Emeritus University of Utah

Easy Publishing Co.

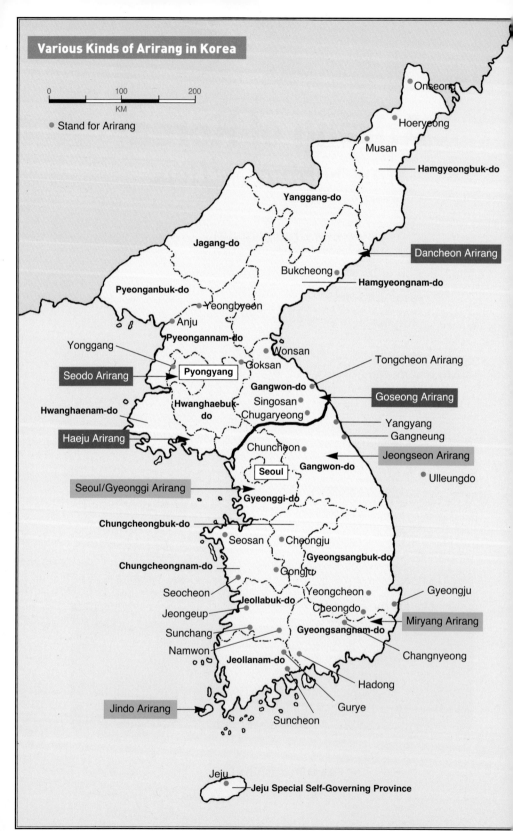

Recomendation

Professor Lee O-young, Former Minister of Culture

Arirang is a song that Korean people have sung from time immemorial. The song is our eternal hearth, a home in our minds, a valued heritage.

Professor Emeritus Lee Chung-myun of the University of Utah is one of them. Touched by the spirit of resistance, harmony, and forgiveness of the Arirang, he has made over three international research trips to sites related to the Arirang. Using the data collected in his travels, he published the first version of Arirang, with the title, *Arirang: Song of Korea*. In it he invoked the concept of consilience, advocated by biologist Edward O. Wilson, as a possible way for developing a comprehensive method of studying Arirang. Now, the new book he wrote, *Arirang of Korea: Han, Sorrows and Hopepe*, adds sections directly from North Korea to his old Arirang.

This book presents the varied emotions of the Korean people, their love for the beautiful melody of this song, and the peace that they uphold. I believe this book will be a great aid to understanding Arirang, to Koreans and to English readers alike.

Now, it is available to the English reader as well. I have no doubt that this will contribute to enhancing the value of the song of Arirang.

Recomendation

Chung Dong-hwa,

Former President of Gyeongin National University of Education

I would like to extend my heartfelt congratulations to Dr. Lee Chung-myun on this publication of *Arirang of Korea: Han, Sorrows and Hopepe.* I cannot hide my joy in that this book also serves as the fulfillment of a lifelong wish of mine as well.

Arirang is an important Korean heritage, a song so representative of Korea that it could almost be argued that Arirang and Korea are synonyms. I had always been saddened that this fact was not being made known throughout the world. However, Professor Lee Chung-myun, an American resident, pulled his elderly body along to the corners of South Korea and even to North Korea. He visited China, Japan, Southeast Asia, South America, and even the Ethnical Koreans in Central Asia to publish his book, Arirang. I can reserve no compliments to attest of his great efforts. I hope that this wonderful opportunity to make Arirang known to the world may serve as a catalyst to the cooling efforts for the reunification of the South and North.

Arirang is a folksong. It was formed by many people throughout a lengthy period of time. No author is known. It is merely estimated that it was composed at around the early Joseon Dynasty. However, Arirang is the sound of the people, unlearned, under oppression, and living a difficult life in poverty.

Arirang is the song of the Korean people, sung by men and women, old and young. In this sense, Arirang can be seen as the naturally produced anthem of Korea, telling the tale of the masses of people who make up the majority of Korea as they overcome their daily hardships. That is why it was also sung for the Asian Games in Busan, and the Sydney Olympic Games, as the athletes and attendees form the South and North joined together as one.

Korea is located in a small corner in the northeast of Asia. We have suffered from countless invasions by China, Mongolia, and the Khitan to the north, and Japan, a maritime power. We have been the arena for their struggles. Furthermore, the common class had to suffer, in addition to foreign invasions, the oppression from the yangban ruling class, as well as poverty and hard work.

Women, in particular, suffered even more greatly under a male-dominated way of life. Their sorrows congealed to form clumps of sadness, or han, and today's Korea was made possible by withstanding such sorrows and not losing hope, according to the author's interpretation. I applaud his superior insight.

Koreans have created a unique culture and have survived through the history of suffering and the oppression of the yangban and the rich. Korea has also achieved a miraculous development, moving from one of the poorest nations in the world to a world leader in record time.

Arirang is the sound that empathizes with a wide range of emotions. It is sad when we hear it while suffering or in difficulty, and powerful and exciting when we are happy and joyful. Japan and China also have their own folksongs, but I believe they do not have one folksong that represents the nation, as Arirang does. This is why even the Japanese praise the Arirang as a world-class folksong.

In today's global age, Arirang is heard in all 150 countries where the Korean diaspora live. In England it is sung as a lullaby, and in the US and Kenya, as a hymn.

The folksong usually has a set melody, and the lyrics change according to the singer. Arirang can also be classified into a few different categories, but the lyrics are countless. Arirang's outstanding characteristic is its refrain.

The main word in the Arirang is the word repeated in the refrain, "Arirang". Among the refrains in the old songs written by the Koreans, there is a popular usage of the vowel sounds "a", "i", and "eo", and the consonant sounds "n", "r", and silent "h". This is evident in the Korean keyboard layout, with the vowels "o", "eo", "a", and "I", and the consonants "a", "h", and "n" are all on the middle row. This indicates that they are used very often.

The vowel "a" is the strongest vowel sound and the "I" is the weakest vowel. The consonant "r" is running water, in other words, the most rhythmical sound. The silent "h" sound is a flap sound, resounding most powerfully. These sounds are ideal for creating a refrain that is both rhythmical and exciting. The "a" + "I" + "a" progression creates a strong-weak-strong rhythm, with the "r" and the silent "h" sound adding to reach the peak of rhythm and excitement.

Due to these characteristics, Arirang, with its repetitions and variations, can be sung easily even by foreigners. This is also why it was recognized as a song with great empathy. I would like to recommend this book to anyone who wants to understand Arirang correctly and showcase Korean culture throughout the world.

Recomendation

Kim Ki-soon, President of Synnara Records Co.

Arirang folksong is, since times immemorial, our nation's song and DNA, and a song of heaven. Also, Arirang is creator's name. It is the song of the spirit, with the heartbeat of the soul and spirit of our people, and wherever we find Korean people, we find the Arirang. One would be hard-pressed to find another example anywhere in the world that represents a nation and is sung by so many people as the Arirang.

Arirang pass leads from sorrow to joy despair to overcoming, darkness to light, suffering to glory, from 4 dimensions to 5-a divide that leads our lives from one place to another. Arirang pass is, on a personal level, a reality that must be overcome in our place in life, whereas on the level of a group of people, it is a history of suffering and despair, and the history of overcoming such setbacks.

Arirang folksong has continued over generations, geographical regions, and ideologies. In order to preserve the Arirang and make it known throughout the world, Synnara Records Co. has made efforts since a long time ago to unearth new data and produce them in recordings. We are making every effort to find and preserve the Arirang, the song of our people, which has been transmitted down the generations from both

South and North. We have also made efforts to meet with everyone interested in this work, to discuss and share ideas, and work for the internationalization of the Arirang.

It was under those circumstances that I met Professor Lee Chung-myun of the University of Utah many times. He also had his own convictions about the Arirang, and was traveling around the world sharing the spirit of the Arirang–resistance, unity, and peace and love through harmony. He is not keeping Arirang pent up within Korea, but working to make it known to the world. His efforts led him to publish the book Arirang in English, as well as Korean, through Easy Publishing Co. This led to his visit to Pyongyang to meet with North Korean Arirang scholars, and a new revised version of the book, tying the South and North as one, was set to be published.

Professor Lee's new revision, *Arirang of Korea: Han, Sorrows and Hopepe*, contains a deep understanding of the Arirang, and shows to the world the humble image, as well as the steel resolve of Korean people and our history. I believe that this book will certainly play a big role in making the Arirang known throughout the world.

Arirang is not merely the song of a nation. Many are working to make it the song of the world, the song of the universe. Synnara Records Co. pledges to work with the scholars making such efforts, with our constant interest and love.

Lastly, I would like to express my gratitude to Professor Lee Chung-myun and Easy Publishing Co. for their efforts.

Recomendation

Walter Jones, University of Utah

I had the honor of working with a combined group of American and Korean Special Forces in the Republic of Korea in 1977. One evening after our exercise was finished, the soldiers gathered at a restaurant to eat and enjoy each other's company for the short period of time that they had left together before the Americans had to return home to the US.

As these Korean and American soldiers spent that evening together, a Korean captain asked the Americans to sing a song that they felt especially good about. So the Americans sang "The Ballad of the Green Berets." The Korean Special Forces soldiers loved this song. They sang it several times in harmony with their American counterparts.

Then an American captain asked his Korean friends to teach the Americans a Korean song. The captain and his subordinates sang a version of "Arirang." It was a very stirring moment. The Americans quickly began to learn the Korean words to this folksong, and the two groups sang it over and over again for nearly one-half hour.

This was an evening in which people from two entirely different parts of the world joined together in friendship and song. It was a wonderful moment. Now that I have read

Professor Lee's manuscript history and explanation of that song, I realize and appreciate more deeply the importance of that night.

"Arirang" expresses very profound emotions. It is not a simple song and, as Professor Lee's writing demonstrates it has many versions and expresses sorrow, hardship, and suffering in a world that is too often a cruel and harsh place to inhabit. But the song gives hope and a ray of light to those who sing it and who commit their spirit to the words and thoughts that it enunciates. It is a great and enduring song.

The manuscript study that he has created is well researched and documented, easy to read, and profound in its demonstrating the importance of "Arirang." I believe that the book that will result from Professor Lee's arduous work will become a classic in Korean historic literature. It will endure, like the song itself, because of its subject and because of Professor Lee's careful and meticulous writing which exudes a love and admiration for Korea and its long and important history as embodied in "Arirang." I will always treasure the opportunity he gave me to read the manuscript. Since Professor Lee has now written his manuscript in English, English-speaking peoples will be able to read the book to enhance their sense of the beauty of Korea and its people and culture. Professor Lee's new book included North Korea intitled *Arirang of Korea : Han, Sorrows and Hopepe* will be widely read in and out of Korea. I am very greatful to the author, Easy Publishing Co. and the employees.

Why did I write the Book?

Lee Chung-myun

On September 15th, 2009, I returned to the University of Utah after publishing an English version of *Arirang: Song of Korea*. A few days later, I received an e-mail from Park Song-il, a diplomat dispatched from Pyongyang to the UN. It can be summarized as follows :

> *I have read your outstanding English version of Arirang: Song of Korea. However, it is regrettable that in your book you omitted North Korea. We would like to ask you to add this portion in your book.*
>
> *If you need any materials, we will send you anything that will help you to complete the job, or we would even like to suggest that you consider visiting Pyongyang and meeting North Korean Arirang scholars to discuss this matter further.*

His e-mail obviously came as a surprise to me. Park, as I later learned, had tried to purchase copies of my book from bookstores throughout the US, but often failed to do this. He eventually contacted me and asked me to sell him five copies.

I immediately obliged.

Instead of just continuing our communication in writing, I thought it would be best to agree with his proposal and visit Pyongyang to meet the Arirang scholars he mentioned. I also wanted to see North Korea with my own eyes. So, with his help, I secured all the necessary documents for entering North Korea, together with my wife, in Autumn 2010. I left the US for Seoul. The next day, I went to the Ministry of Unification to inform them of my schedule for the trip to the North. They advised me to visit alone because of the recent complications that resulted from the Yeonpyeongdo Incident.

In light of this, I decided to change my original 3-week plan in North Korea to 1-week. My North Korea travel agent in the US said that it would be difficult to alter the itinerary, and I would need to plan the trip for another time. It was a great pity that I should return to the US with the feeling that the road to Pyongyang was so near and yet so far. "Professor Lee and Mrs. Lee have a wonderful time in Pyongyang". Park's voice still echoed in my mind.

A few weeks later, I called and e-mailed him in New York to let him know what had happened, but there was no response. I thought he had already returned to Pyongyang, and I regretted not being able to say goodbye to him. He had done so much to help me visit North Korea.

In 2011, I called the North Korea Mission to the UN. However, the voice answering the phone was not that of Park

Song-il. It was that of Park Chul, a newly dispatched diplomat. He said that Park Song-il had returned to the Pyongyang and that he was his replacement, adding that he would be in charge of my future plans to visit to North Korea. He also noted the close relationship that Mr. Park Song-il and I had developed and promised to do his best to ensure that I would be able to visit Pyongyang soon. He even said that I might have a chance to watch a performance of Arirang Mass Games while there.

He was very considerate, to say the least. I gave my word that I would wait for reunification after I complete writing the Korean and English version of Arirang combining sources from the two Koreas. After receiving all the necessary papers from Seoul and North Korea, I visited Pyongyang from the last week of September until mid October 2011.

Arriving at Sunan International Airport, in Pyongyang, was an absolutely unforgettable moment. Everything seemed dreadful and I wondered to myself whether this is a place I would like to visit again after reunification.

I was assigned room 22 of the Koryo Hotel. My schedule started the day after my arrival with a morning walk along the Daedonggang River. It looked like it would turn out to be very productive. After my walk I visited Kim Il-sung University and a number of historic sites in Pyongyang.

Then I met Professor Moon Song-yop, Professor/Director of the Folklore Research Institute, Kong Myong-song, Professor Yun Su-dong, Professor Moon said that Professor Um Ha-jin, who was absent from the gathering, had recently assumed the position of Dean of the College of Music so could not attend the meeting.

We had an informal talk about the following :

① The status of the Song of Arirang
② Arirang Symposium in 2012
③ Theoretical approach for Arirang Studies / Arirangology
④ Underlying notions among Hyanga, Manyoshu
   (a collection of poems), and folksongs(including Arirangs)
⑤ Aewonseong and Susimga and Arirang

During the meeting, I suggested a regular South-North joint Arirang Symposium in order to establish a global network related to the Study of Arirang, including the establishment of Arirangology. Everybody in the meeting agreed with this.

This informal talk turned out to be a great success and we all agreed to see each other every year in Pyongyang, Seoul, or Beijing. Before closing this informal talk, we talked about the English version of my book of Arirang. We agreed that the book should be completed by 2012.

Upon returning to the US, I explained to Park Chul in New York what had happened in Pyongyang. He was also very happy to hear the fortunate results. But as it is often said, the good news comes with the bad. A future joint symposium on Arirang looks unlikely in 2012 because of the ongoing changes in the Korean

Peninsula.

Despite this, I did my best to publish the book in 2012 just as I had promised in Pyongyang. To achieve this, I attempted to visit North Korea again in mid April 2012 to gather more materials and exchange views with some of the Professors there, but plans for this trip fell through. Instead, I independently continued my research and kept my word that I would published an English version of *Arirang of Korea: Han, Sorrows and Hopepe* that combined South and North Korea together as one country. Nothing is more important to me than letting the whole world know about "Arirang", a song that embodies the spirit and history of all Korean people.

In completing this project, Park Chul and Park Song-il did their best to provide an opportunity for this book. On the way I called Park Chul several time to get relevant data to speed up this job. He never denied me any requests for help. He was always willing to help this project, and because of this, it was possible to complete this taxing job without fail. I was able to publish this book only because of the enthusiastic help I received from these two diplomats.

I would like to express my gratitude to Professor Lee O-young, Former President Chung Dong-hwa, President Kim Ki-soon and my colleagues in the department of Geography at the University of Utah. SawooHoe in Salt Lake City.

Also to President of Easy Publishing Co. Suh Yong-soon who has done so much to aid my efforts to publish Arirang that combined versions from both South and North Korea. Coporation Ecopeace Asia Director General Lee Samuel thougshtfully arranged my field trip in Central Asia relating to Korean forced Misration in 1937.

And Hwang Chi-young, Professor Lee Dong-chun, Professor Emeritus Park Doo-bok, Dr. Kim Joon and his wife Na Ki-joung, Professor Song Jong-hun, Yoo young-whee, Director Lee Chor-u, Park Tae-Jin, Kang Jin-seok, Park Sung-hyun, Yoon In-seop and Yeon Heung-sook for editing, and proofreading drafts of this book and providing notes.

Also, Dr. Lee Doh-yeel and his team in Michigan, Christine E. S. Lee in Chicago and Dr. Lee Andrew K. C. and his team in Washington D.C.

Last, but not least, I would like to thank to my wife Kim Ul-la who has encouraged me to write this book and put up with all the difficulties it presented.

Contents

Chapter 1 Introduction

Chapter 2 The Song of Arirang After my Heart

Chapter 3 The Origin of the Song of Arirang

Chapter 4 The Story of Han and Arirang

Chapter 5 The Film Arirang

Chapter 6 The Major Types of Arirang

Chapter 7 The Diffusion of Arirang

Chapter 8 People's Love of Arirang

Chapter 9 Song of Arirang in the Hymn and Lullaby

Chapter 10 Similarity of Arirang

Introduction

Sunrising on the top of Mt. Mindungsan(Jeongseon)

1

Chapter

1. Arirang : Past, Present and Future

When someone raises the question "What is the representative Korean folksong and flower in Korea?", people will answer without hesitation, they are doubtlessly the song of Arirang and Mugunghwa (the Rose of Sharon flower). A folksong is a song which honestly expresses the common people's true feeling. The folksong does not need tricks and subjects. It is not for those who are highly educated.

The folksong does not stick to historical facts. It does not have to be woven with beautiful and graceful words. The life of the folksong does not need any authority. We can call it a folksong if it reveals the gentle and mild emotion in the common people's hearts. It is one of the first steps of the intellectual activity in human history. Also, it originated from the first artistic pulse. Thus, the folksong is regarded as the song of the common people and it reflected the people of all social standings of the times.

Accordingly, we may assume that those who engraved an object on the rock in the Old Stone Age certainly had a sense of art, too. Also, they enjoyed (producing) the correct sounds of human voice (rhythm) as well as physical rhythm based upon these types of behavior. We may surmise that dance and song existed from the beginning of human history.

Therefore, regardless of race or nation, people performed dance and sang folksongs. If we search for the origin of the culture, it will be the folksong.

In this respect, Korea was surely the country of the folksong. Before the invention of written characters, there was song. The song was only one of the lyrical types of music for primitive people.

Johann G. Herder (1744-1803) was a German philosopher, theologian, poet and literary critic. He is associated with the periods of enlightenment like "Sturm und Drang" and "Weimer Classicism." He coined the word of 'Volkslied'. He thought that community plays a more important role than lineage. It means that listening to the population's voice, one realizes what the population wants. Therefore the country can advance to their proper direction for the future of the nation.

2. The Folksong of Korea

In Korea there were the folksongs existed since the earlier period. Especially, people of the Silla Kingdom enjoyed their bountiful life and magnanimous freedom. They had a lot of folksong. During the Silla Kingdom period the people amplified their culture. Among other things, music prospered and a special government office was set up in charge of music to accompany court rituals. The folksong, in a sense, was a voice of the common people and also it reflected the history of culture.

According to Samguksagi, the 51st Queen, Jinseong ordered through Wihong and Daegu to collect the Hyangga (native songs of old Korean folksong) from all over the country under her rule. And it was compiled in 888, and named Samdaemok (the collection of old Korean folksong) in Korea. Also, as the poetry related to high society, we may list King Yuri of the Goguryeo Kingdom who wrote Hwangjoga (love story).

In the Silla Kingdom, Queen Jindeok wrote Taepyeongsong to celebrate the coronation of the Emperor in the Tang Dynasty.

They were written in Chinese characters. However, folksong mainly belong to lower class, so-called the common people. So they contained many slang expressions, which made people treat the folksong with little care. That's why few remains of Hyangga are used in performing religious services such as praying to God or celebrating the completion of religious buildings. However, the form and text of the Hyangga gradually changed and came to resemble the Chinese music style when the letter and thought of China were introduced to Korea. Thus, Hyangga gradually drifted from the original one. As a result, the national style of Hyangga faded away.

On the other hand, another group of folksongs drew more and more popular attention. They did not care about the style or the morals of Confucianism. Furthermore, they did not follow the thought of non-interference of Taoism and Buddhism. Based on the optimism of Korean people, the folksong thrived. Korean folksongs survived the cultural invasion from China as the folksong was well protected by the common people.

Upon the introduction of Chinese culture, two types of social structure emerged in Korea. One eagerly pursued the characteristics of Korean style and supported traditional spirit in Korea. People of this class did not have political and intellectual power. They didn't belong to high society. They were regarded as the lower class of the common people. In a sense they were strong supporters of the folksong. While the high society class was busy memorizing the old Chinese poems of the Han and Wei Dynasty in China, the lower class people were eager to upgrade the national spirit. They stood strongly as the protector of national art. One of their fundamental strongholds was the folksong.

In the Joseon Dynasty there was Emperor Gojong who was interested in lyrical lines of musical performance. Whenever festivals were held at the palace, he invited musical groups and also encouraged farmers to sing work songs.

The writer Lee Gwang-su made a comment on the folksong in his article entitled *A Some Considerations on Folksong!* He said the folksong has kept essential elements of Korean culture which have not been influenced by outside factors. He continued saying that the folksong of Korea had a unique sense, rhythm and sentiment. He thought, therefore, that the folksong of Korea had immense value. He suggested, based upon this, that we should inject our value into the new style poetry. Lee's comment was meaningful and productive as well as instructive. It was the first suggestion on the study of the folksong in Korea.

3. The Characteristics of Folksong in Korea

Korean people are warm and simple hearted. They also have an unspoiled mind and sing daily. They have no extraordinary desire or want. Nor is, there any trick intended to warp the folksong. Instead, they demonstrate their good natured mentality in gestures when they sing the song. This gesture is similar to that found in Manyoshu of Muromachi period in Japan.

The Korean folksong is delicate yet simple, frank, yet lively. Furthermore, the song is the expression of Korean people's nature and feelings of daily life and genuine emotion. Simply put, it is the common people's ballad.

Japanese folksongs are delicate, graceful and beautiful. However, the Korean folksong has simplicity, frankness, vividness, strength. The folksong of Korea is dynamic, innocent and unpolished. The folksong is easy to sing for common people. These are the characteristics of Korea's folksong. They make the folksong the nation's song forever.

The folksong Arirang shows all aspects of human lives like

love, agony, grudge, envy, sorrow, joy, life and death. Even though the famous folksong Hyangga and Manyoshu would become extinct, Arirang will always be sung by Korean people within and without. The folksong Arirang will continue as the Korean folksong while standing on the characteristics of the song of Arirang: containing cooperative spirit and resistance to injustice and forgiveness. Although Chinese and Japanese politically governed the Korean, only the folksong remain untouched. The folksong of Korea clung to the spirit of Korea.

There are two types of folksong. One is quickly disappeared while the other is long-lived. This type of folksong has a thought to take a breath. For the Korean people, Arirang meant their thought and life. Throughout history it protected the Korean people. Arirang is not just a folksong. Beyond time (age) and thought, it expresses sympathy with a Korean people's view. That's why Arirang should be kept and passed to our descendants as the property of Korean people. Arirang is the greatest common message for Korean people. Kitahara Hakushu made a comment on the folksong of the Korea. He said it is much more passionate due to Korean nationality. It is more cynical, and has more grief and emotion than that of Japan.

Kim Ji-yeon, a expert of Arirang indicated that the Korean folksong expresses the pure emotion of Korean people without decoration. Also, he described the origin of Folksong. It appeared in Samguksagi describing various people such as

Buyeo, Mahan, Jinhan. These people danced and spent a wonderful time singing like the birds in the mountains. Also, in the documents Houhanshu Dongyizhuan, it read that Dongyizu (an alias for Korean people) enjoyed themselves drinking and singing. Also Kim summarized the characteristics of the folksong of Korea as follows:

① It is anonymous
② open to sympathy
③ and has social mobility, and
④ the local color and the feature of each period
⑤ formed with melody

One of the significant reasons for the development of Korean folksong was the people who knew the song most intimately were commoners. People used the folksong as one of the outlets of their sorrow and helpless status. Especially during the Japanese colonization, Korean people resisted Japanese occupation openly or secretly and used the folksong as a significant tool to this effect.

4. The Features of the Folksong by Region

Choe Nam-seon summarized briefly the characteristic style of the Korean folksong by region.

① Yeongnam style : Yeongnam refers to Gyeongsangbuk-do and Gyeongsangnam-do Provinces. The folksong of Yeongnam was marked by a vigorous, overpowering and very dynamic style.

② Honam style : Honam refers to Jeollabuk-do and Jeollanam-do Provinces. The Honam style was described as gentle and comfortable.

③ Gyeonggi style : The folksongs of this area are marked as graceful and elegant. Some of them are the royal court style.

④ Seodo style : This includes Pyeongan-do and Hwanghae-do Provinces whose style was sad and sorrowful.

Along this line, Isabella Bird made a comment on the songs of Asia. She said Asian folksongs are mostly sorrowful, but the

Korean folksongs were the most sorrowful. Is there any approach combining the modern and traditional aspects together to lead a new approach to Korean culture? If the modern countries lose the sense of sovereignty and independence immediately, they will fall into the new type of cultural colonization. Because of this, we must try to keep our traditional culture. This attitude will preserve our invaluable culture without failure.

In the past, the spread of the folksong was slow and confined to local areas. Also, the scope of activity of the people was limited. Thus, the spread of the folksong was limited and stagnated due to the inconvenience of transportation. Today, however, thanks to the rapid development of the transportation system, new styles of folksong flow into our society whether we like it or not. If it disturbs the beauty and nature of the Korean folksong, we must firmly stand and protect our cultural values: the lively feelings and true emotion of a straightforward and innocent Korean people.

The Song of Arirang After my Heart

Pasqueflower of Donggang River, special production in Korea(Jeongseon)

2
Chapter

1. My Boyhood(Jatgogae)

My earliest Arirang memory begins with my boyhood in my hometown, Gwangju, South Korea. I used to collect fire wood all day with my older brother to help my parents. I had to go over a pass called Jatgogae. The pass always reminded me of Arirang. There are several reasons why I remembered the Arirang Pass. First, I often had to avoid the pass because there were always forest rangers confiscating the fire wood. My detour of the pass reflected my hardship as a 6-year-old boy.

Also, there was a small tavern-like place around the pass area. I often encountered many people from the place passing by. Some people expressed their sadness by singing local folk-songs such as Arirang.

Others were singing their small accomplishments and their happiness. Such expression of the local people during my boyhood also reminded me of my early association with Arirang. Of course, I can not find any trace of my old pass the way I remembered.

Arirang Pass(Jatgogae) in my hometown

The Jatgogae area has been completely developed and filled with cars and shopping streets. Even though my old pass has vanished, my memory with the pass played a critical role in shaping what I am and who I am now. The pass of my boyhood was the very beginning of my Arirang story.

2. The Koreans in Manchuria
by W. T. Cook

In 1957, I was a graduate student in the Geography Department at the University of Michigan in Ann Arbor, Michigan. One day a book entitled *The Koreans in Manchuria* got my attention at the library. The author, W. T. Cook, a faculty member of Christian College in Manchuria, described the Korean migrants lives there in the northeastern part of modern China.

W. T. Cook (1878-1952) belonged to the Presbyterian Missionary of the US. His Korean name was Guk Yu-chi. He was dispatched by the North headquarter of the Presbyterian denomination. He arrived in Korea with his wife Maude Hempill as a missionary. At first, he was engaged in missionary work at Cheongju, Chungcheongbuk-do Province. Later in 1917, he did missionary work at Andong, Gyeongsangbuk-do Province.

In 1918, he switched missionary work to Seoncheon, Pyeonganbuk-do Province. Still later he was dispatched in charge of missionary work for the Korean people in

Manchuria. Especially, his activity was concentrated in the Mudanjiang and Changchun areas of Manchuria. Cook's missionary work was influential. He cared for the Korean people who migrated from Korea. Cook worked as the head of the Presbyterian Church there. Thus, he had an opportunity to observe the life of Koreans in Manchuria. He vividly described how Koreans migrated to the region. Here is the paraphrased version of his remark:

They crossed over the icy cold river during winter. There were around 40 to 50 people in a group. They walked along the hill to find a place to settle.

Cook also noted that Koreans were singing Korean songs in their struggle. One of their songs was likely Arirang. In regard to Cook's observations, some criticized the author for exaggerating the living conditions of Korean people. Such claims were derived from speculation that Cook attempted to get financial aid from the religious foundations in New York. However, I found his description of the Korean people's life impartial and persuasive.

The deplorable living conditions of Koreans in Manchuria were also substantiated by Japanese scholars during the Japanese occupation. For instance, Yanaihara Tadao, the President of Tokyo University, sharply criticized the implementation of the Japanese colonial policy toward Korea.

3. Song of Arirang
   at the University of Malaya

From 1967 to 1970, I served as a visiting Professor in the Department of Geography at the University of Malaya. There were not many Koreans there in those days. The former president of the Republic of Korea, Choi Kyu-hah was the Korean Ambassador to Malaysia. There were about 200 Korean medical doctors.

I still fondly remember my days with Pai Su-dong in the Surgical Department and Lee Dong-sik in the Anesthesia Department at the University of Malaya. We stayed at same resident house of the University.

One day I conducted field work in the Penang area with my students. It took us several hours to arrive at the survey area. While travelling, in order to kill monotonous time in the buses, I taught my students how to sing Arirang to make the long ride more fun. I explained the stories behind Arirang: Namely, that the folksong has a long history with Korean sorrow and pride. Surprisingly, the students quickly learned the melody in Korean.

After 3 years of my tenure, I accepted an offer for a Visiting Professor at California State University, Fresno. The student body of the Department of Geography in Malaya organized a farewell party for me.

The party was memorable in many aspects, especially because they sang Arirang that they learned from the Penang field trip. All the students stood up and began to sing the song of Arirang in Korean accompanied by a professional musical band. Thus, the song of Arirang echoed around the campus. They sang Arirang over and over. I still miss the hospitality of the Malaysian people, the student body and their farewell song of Arirang.

4. Korean Migration to the Intermountain West, US

Under the Japanese occupation period (1910-1945) Korean people shed tears singing the song of Arirang. Between the 1920's and the 1930's, large numbers of people moved out to Manchuria, Russia and the US. In the 1930s, a great numbers of migrants moved to Hawaii in order to work in the sugar plantation farms. But the Koreans were not happy about their job. Some returned to Korea and others went to the mainland city of San Francisco for a better life. A few of them headed to the Intermountain West for mining jobs. Thus the early Koreans spread out over the mining area in the Intermountain West, US.

The University of Utah offered me a post of professorship in the Department of Geography in July 1972. Since then I have spent a lot of time studying the Korean migration into the Intermountain West. (Utah, Wyoming, Colorado, etc.) Many Korean mining workers, like others at the time were subjected to the dangers of the mining industry and perished in mining explosions.

Korean miners killed in accidents were buried in the graveyard of the mining companies. My research was aimed at learning about Korean mining victims. The specific information I was interested in included name, departure route from Korea, hometown, mining site, date of death, and income.

In order to get the data my team of researchers contacted the local museum and library. Obtaining the information initially was very difficult because the officials of the museum and historical library told me that there were no Korean miner in their records. They claimed that most of victims were Chinese or Japanese. However, I asked them to show me their documents for verification.

Upon my request, the officials granted me and my associates the access to the documents. To our and their surprise, we found the typical last name of Korean such as Kim, Lee, Park or Hong. We used the same approach to Korean migration study whenever we visited the mining companies in the Intermountain West-Utah, Wyoming, Colorado areas.

I would like to share the story of Yoo Kong-wu who is buried at the Castle Gate Cemetery, Carbon County, Utah. We found his grave site in 2000. His grave stone was engraved with the following information : Yoo Kong-wu, born in 1872 died in March 8, 1924 due to the explosion of mining. Hometown is Kyungido, Pochun, Korea (currently Pocheon,

Koreans visit yoo's graveyard to pay their respects at the Castle gate graveyard

Gyeonggo-do, Korea). Based upon our information, the Korean Broadcasting System(KBS) arranged for Yoo's grandson to visit Yoo's grave site. His grandson brought a handful of soil from his grandmother's grave in Yoo's hometown in Korea. He scattered the soil over Yoo's grave, and wiped the tombstone with towel. his grandson felt that he symbolically made a proper burial ritual for his grandfather by scattering Korean soil. This reunion brought happiness and sadness to all of US.

We contacted KBS to explain about my project and Yoo's story in 2001. KBS used this occasion and our project on Korean migration to honor the 100th year of US-Korean migration. A KBS team came to Utah to report on Korean migration and Yoo's story. KBS found out that Yoo had about 100 descendents. There are many other unknown Korean mining workers who died in the Intermountain West. Many Korean miners who perished must have gone through various physical and emotional hardships.

I would not be surprised to find that they found comfort singing and listening to Arirang because it was the most popular and widespread song in Korea.

5. *Song of Ariran* by Kim San and Nym Wales

I read the original version in English of *Song of Ariran[sin]* by Kim San and Nym Wales published in 1941 at the John Day Company, New York. I also read the Japanese version (translated by Ando Jiro) and Korean version (translated by Jo Uh-wa). It was remarkable that Nym Wales grasped the history of Korea and Kim's life as a revolutionary for just one short summer in China. She originally was assigned to cover the International Communist Party at Yan'an in 1937 but she could not make her assignment because the conference was cancelled. Instead, she visited the Lu Xun Library for her readings. She found that the books she wanted were checked out by a Korean named Kim San.

This unusual circumstance led her to meet Kim. Nym Wales had a good impression of Kim and learned about him as a communist revolutionary in China. She made seven notebooks about him and published the book of *Song of Ariran* through the John Day Company. However, the US Government banned the book because it contained communism. The book was the story of

Kim's experience as a young revolutionary in China. The topic includes his guerrilla warfare, imprisonment, love story, marriage and underground campaign.

The book cover of Song of Ariran

On November 20, 1930 Kim San was arrested and sent to Tianjin, China. The conversation between Kim San and a police officer showed Kim San's feeling and affection toward *Song of Ariran*. Also the Japanese police officer was touched by this conversation. Let me quote the conversation :

The plainclothes policeman with me was a graduate of Waseda University, one of prestigious universities in Japan. He asked me about my experience in prison "Prison is the greatest college of humanity," I said. "What did you learn there?" "I learned that I have great force within myself. I like Koreans very much," the policeman remarked confidentially "and my present wife is Korean" He asked if I sing a Korean song. "There is only one song I can sing on a day like this," I remarked. "What is that?" "It is an old, old Korean song of death of defeat-Song of Ariran." I told him the meaning of the song and sang it. He enjoyed song very much. "I'll never forget it," he promised warmly and called for some beer which we drank together.

In Korea we have a folksong, a beautiful ancient song which was created out of the living heart of a suffering people. It is sad, as all deep-felt beauty is sad. It is tragic, as Korea has for so long been tragic. Because it is beautiful and tragic it has been the favorite song of all Koreans for three hundred years. Near Seoul is a hill called the Pass of Ariran. During the oppressive Joseon Dynasty there was a giant solitary pine at the top of this hill, and this was the official place of execution for several hundred years. Tens of thousands of prisoners were hanged until dead on a gnarled branch of that ancient tree, their bodies suspended over a cliff at the side. Some were bandits. Some were common criminals. Some were dissident scholars. Some were political and family enemies of the emperor. Many were poor farmers who had raised their hands against oppression. Many were rebel youths who had struggled against tyranny and injustice. The story is that one of those young men composed a song during his imprisonment, and as he trudged slowly up the Pass of Ariran, he sang this song. The people learned it, and after that whenever a man was condemned to die he sang this in farewell to his joys or sorrows. Every Korean prison echoes with these haunting notes, and no one dares deny a man's death-right to sing it at *the end. Song of Ariran has come to symbolize the tragedy of Korea. Its meaning is symbolic of constantly climbing over obstacles only to find death at the end. It is a song of death and not of life. But death is not defeat. Out of many deaths, victory may be born. There are those of us who would write another verse for this ancient Song of Ariran. *That last verse is not yet written. We are many dead, and many more have "crossed the Yalu River" into exile. But our return will not be long in the future.*

Lastly, I quote the folksong; also they listed a sad and sorrowful stanza of the song of Arirang in the opening chapter of a book as follows :

Song of Ariran(Old Korean folksong of exile and prison and national humiliation)
*Ariran : Pronounced with broad a and accented on the last syllable, thus, A-ree-ran.

Ariran, Ariran, Arari O!
Crossing the hills of Ariran
There are twelve hills of Ariran
And now I am crossing the last hills

Many stars in the deep sky
Many crimes in the life of man

Ariran, Ariran, Arari O!
Crossing the hills of Ariran

Ariran is the mountain of sorrow
And the path to Ariran has no returning
Ariran, Ariran, Arari O!
Crossing the hills of Ariran

Oh, twenty million countrymen, where are you now?
Alive are only three thousand ri**, of mountains and rivers
Ariran, Ariran, Arari O! Crossing the hills of Ariran
Now I am an exile crossing the Yalu River
And the mountains and rivers of three thousand ri are also
lost
Ariran, Ariran, Arari O!
Crossing the hills of Ariran

** ri is Korean traditional length unit.

As we briefly examined Kim San's life through a few stories, Song of Ariran reflects the life of the Korean people in modern history.

6. The Eight Major Home Grounds of the Song of Arirang

I have spent more than 50 years of my life outside of Korea. These places were Malaysia, Japan and the US where I have studied and taught. During this period, I have encountered both sad and happy occasions. However, I feel I have always made positive progress through my happy and sad life as I have always put myself at ease through Arirang. This often brings good memories of my old friends in Korea. Upon my retirement from the University of Utah December 2002, I decided to visit the birthplaces of Arirang: Seoul/Gyeonggi, Jeongseon, Miryang and Jindo. It was ironic that I had never paid a visit to the cited places even though I have had numerous field trips because of my education and teaching in geography.

First, I visited Jeongseon, the cradle of the song of Arirang. The layout of the town was beautiful because of its natural beauty and beautification. Locals are simple, humble and friendly. It occurred to me that they were not spoiled at all.

During the Joseon Dynasty, Yi Jung-hwan, a famous human geographer, described the human and natural environment of the Jeongseon area in his book *Taengniji* as follows :

Anyone who walk into the Jeongseon area, he can not see blue sky and can not meet people on the pass over. It was lonely and remote place with deep forest, the high blue sky, the winding stream, and the breeze.

I read one article in which Kim Yeol-gyu (former Professor at Sogang University) described his experiences in Jeongseon. Professor Kim expressed his admiration for the natural beauty and the genuine people in this area. Having visited the hometown of the song of Arirang, I could appreciate his applause for the region.

From 1972 to 1980, I employed remote sensing technique to study land cover change. This technique used the application of satellite data to survey specific areas without physical contact. I thought that the marvelous tool would do many wonders in the field of land use. With this new tool, I produced exciting research data that I presented to the international geographical congress held in Paris, France in 1983.

Adopting these techniques, I conducted land use mapping on Jeju Special Self-Governing Province, Mokpo in Korea, and other areas in the US. Based upon those techniques, I wrote papers and presented them at many International Geographical Congresses. However, experience from my field work in the hometown of the song of Arirang was not comparable to that of my excitement about the application of remote sensing technique.

I believe that Arirang plays a much more significant role in my life than that of any other professional path I have been through.

The Origin of the
Song of Arirang

A rain fog of Joyanggang River(Jeongseon)

3

Chapter

The song of Arirang has a long history in Korea. This song has not only the spirit but also all emotions of Koreans. Therefore, if there is a Korean, Arirang must be there with him or her. However, it is really difficult to answer the question of "What is Arirang?" I can't leave this question in abeyance, because the question must be a profound issue for Korean. I would try to give a better understanding of Arirang to the readers.

First of all, I would like to focus on the origin of Arirang and the Arirang Pass. There is no certain definition or origin of Arirang. A few scholars suggest the views which they comprehend. According to Kim Yeon-gap, an expert of Arirang, the song of Arirang reflects the complex emotions and lives of Koreans. It preserves the wisdom, customs, wishes and social conditions of the past. Certainly, Arirang contains complex emotions, and then it expresses straightforwardly the soul of Korean people.

In the song of Arirang, there is always an Arirang Pass.

What is the Arirang Pass? What does it stand for? First, the pass is an intersection of apprehension and hope on the road to enter the unknown world. Korean traditional society regarded a pass as a boundary of each village. So the pass worked as an interchange among villages. And crossing the pass means "farewell." And also, ancients compared the pass with life. Kim San (I discussed about him in a previous section) described that "Arirang Pass is twelve passes. That is, life is a series of afflictions and trials. The Arirang Pass in our life becomes the history of suffering and conquest as well." Arirang Pass can be called the "division" which marks the change from sorrow to joy and from darkness to brightness. All the songs of Arirang say "going to pass the hill," but never say "what happened after passing."

After all, Arirang Pass seems to mean a real life, which people should conquer. Shinmura Ezru, Japanese, defined that the Arirang Pass of Korea existed as not a reality but a tale on the dictionary *Kojijen*. Therefore, Arirang Pass has many meanings, and is everywhere. Consequently, Arirang Pass is in our mind. This is the reason he mentioned "the pass nonexistent on the map." One Arirang Pass is located in Inatsuki Machi, Fukuoka Prefecture in Japan. During the Japanese colonial period, Korean conscript workers used to live there. And now Japanese have called this city an Arirang Pass since that time.

1. Who Created the Song of Arirang?

Regarding the origin of the song of Arirang, there are many tales. There are two historic sites near Gyeongju, where was the capital of the Silla Kingdom. One is a well nearby Seokguram (a grottoed Buddhist temple) established in the 8th century on the slopes of Mt. Tohamsan, which contains a monumental statue of the Buddha. Its name is Aryeongjeong. The other is a stream running close to Bulguksa (a Buddhist temple built in 774) and its name is the Aryeongcheon Stream. A rough high hill is located between the two. The pass was named Arirang Pass. It was not easy for Silla people to cross the pass.

On the way side, a girl was drawing water from the Aryeongjeong (well) and saw a knight sitting by the Aryeongcheon Stream to sharpen his sword. She fell in love with the knight at first sight, and then sang the song of Arirang with yearning for him.

2. Folksong of the Joseon Dynasty : Arirang

Whenever Koreans talk about beautiful songs in their country, they name Arirang with no hesitation. The Arirang is one of the most popular lyric folksongs in Korea. Around the 20th century, Arirang spread out nationwide. Furthermore, after a long time Arirang crossed the region and over the border, to everywhere Koreans live.

Arirang has maintained its long historical origin. Various origins are known to the Korean people at the present. "Seongbu and Yi Rang" is representative of one of the tales presented.

In the middle of the Joseon Dynasty (1392-1910) in Gyeonggi-do Province, a couple named Seongbu and Yi Rang served as servants in the house of Kim Jae-su. One day they participated in a community riot, so they were chased by the government troops. In order to escape from the chase, they went into the hilly area where no one lived.

They were happy together for a while. However after a while, Yi Rang was determined to go back and support their comrades. The people in the village were having a hard time due to the high tax imposed by the local authorities and the merciless land owners.

Under these circumstances, the poor common people worked out the plan to stage the riot. Thus Yi Rang parted with his wife, Seongbu and crossed over the pass to go to the battleground.

The wife, Seongbu was left alone. She waited for Yi Rang to return. She could not help crying at parting, so she sang a song "If you leave me alone, you could not go far and would have sore feet." She waited for her husband to return home for 3 years. She missed him every day singing 'Arirang' and watching the pass he crossed. The song she sang spread by word of mouth and it has become Arirang today.

Besides, there are a lot of other theories relating to the origin and the history of Arirang. Those were squeezed into the tales of the reconstruction of Gyeongbokgung Palace in Seoul. It was a big project run by Daewongun(the father of the young King Gojong and the regent, 1820-1898). He needed a great deal of money as well as labor.

At first, the government collected money from the rich classes only, but later, as money was running short, they began to collect money from the poor common people. It was not voluntary but compulsory to. So the people complained "I wish I was deaf," and then I could not hear the order. Someone said that the origin of Arirang came from the A-i-rong(meaning being deaf).

Some say that Arirang came from Ananni(being unable to leave). The pronunciation of Ananni was not comfortable to Koreans so they modified the word into Arinan. Finally, it became Arirang. Others say the words of Arirang were derived from Arirang which means 'I miss my lover.'

3. Other Sources

When did people begin to sing Arirang? There are so many different opinions and theories. Although the song of Arirang has been sung for a long time, I regret that there is not one generally accepted theory. I would like to mention several sources as follows:

a. Aryeong

Park Hyeokgeose and Aryeong, the King and the Queen of Silla traveled all around the country to encourage the people to farm and to raise silkworms. So the people praised the Queen, and they sang for her. Someone suggests that the song of Arirang was derived from the song for her. This theory provides a basis for similar pronunciation between her name, "Aryeong" and "Arirang."

b. The Pass of Arirang

The words of the folksong Arirang have changed through time. However, the musical refrain never changed and the tune (melody) has been always sad and sorrowful. The song of Arirang always mentioned Arirang Pass. Some people wonder whether it might be the name of a place or a person. Due to the road situation, those who wanted to go south had to cross over the northern part of Jabiryeong in Pyeongan-do Province today. People have identified it as Arirang Pass.

On the other hand, there is a big argument regarding the pronunciation of Angnang among scholars. The two most leading pronunciations are Nangnang and Angnang. I support the Angnang theory. Angnang appeals because there was a place named Angnang in ancient Korea. Examining Arirang and Ara we may assume that Arirang or Ara related with Ara or Ala. Whenever there was a political change, the native people used to move south ward to seek safety. People left the homeland and moved toward south to reach the borderline. Then they crossed over the pass so-called Arirang Pass. By that time they felt sad and sorrowful. Then, they began to sing the song for comfort from their hardships. I assume that Arirang derived from the ancient old Korea because the melody is so sad.

Yang Ju-dong, who was a scholar on Korean literature, analyzed the origin through etymology. He said that Arirang meant the pass of Ariyeong with suggesting passes of the whole country. To explain in detail, when the ancients migrated from North to the Korean Peninsular crossing a high mountain, they were fully exposed to the bright spot on the top of the mountain. Thus, they named the pass "Ari." Ari means "brightness". Crossing the pass of Ari, they sang a song about their difficult situation. This could be one of the origins of Arirang.

c. A-Mi-Il-Yeong

As the Joseon Dynasty was coming to the end, the country was turbulent, so the powers of the world wanted to acquire Korea. At that time, Koreans warned themselves of the powers such as Russia(A), America(Mi), Japan(Il), and British (Yeong).

d. Meari(mountain echo)

This theory came from Gangwon-do Province. The province is surrounded by high mountains. The residents of Gangwon-do have characteristics of inhabitants of a mountainous district. They grew familiar with echo (Meari in Korean). "Me" means mountain, and ari means a sound or a song. And then, ari became Arirang today.

e. Ko Kwon-sam and Arirang

I would like to discuss Arirang philosophy of Ko Kwon-sam, a korean political scientists. I came to know him while I was an undergraduate student at the College of Education, Seoul National University in 1946. My impression of him was that he didn' t behave like an important college professor. He was quiet and reserved. He walked with his head down carrying the same bag all the time. Yet, I still recall him as a philosopher with deep thoughts. To my surprise, he developed and established his own authority on the song of Arirang's role in Korean history and culture during the Japanese occupation period.

Information on Professor Ko was very limited since he was presumed to have been abducted to North Korea during the Korea War in 1950. I found very few facts about him through my research on him. He was born in Seongsan, a small village on Jejudo Island in Korea. He was from a noble family. In 1927, he graduated from Waseda University, one of the prestigious universities in Japan. He majored in political science and conducted research at the same institute after the graduation.

He also worked as a member of the civil movement for Korea in Osaka, Japan. He organized a similar civil movement in his hometown. Because of his involvement with this activity, he was under the constant surveillance of Japanese authorities. After Korea was liberated from Japan, he served as a faculty at Dongguk University and Seoul National University. Because of his philosophy on Arirang, I feel that my encounter with him does not seem to be of mere chance or luck. I am very fortunate to bring his 'Airong' philosophy into Arirang.

He expressed his view on Arirang in his book of *The Rise and Fall of the Recent Joseon Dynasty* published in 1933. He attempted to publish his research on Arirang, but the GGJ banned this. After the Korean liberation from Japan, he shared his work on Arirang through his book, *Joseon Political History* published in Osaka, Japan in 1947. His discussion on 'Airong' philosophy revealed that "Airong" was superior to that of Mahatma Gandhi's Satyagraha, a philosophy of non-violent resistance in Sanskrit.

"Airong" idea was described in his article, *Joseon Political History*. He initially assumed that Arirang had nothing to do with political systems, but later, he realized that he had misunderstood the role of Arirang in politics. Ko also pointed out that the birth of Arirang was at the beginning of the Joseon Dynasty (1392-1910). The time coincides with that of the Renaissance in 14th and 17th century Europe. He pointed out the similarity of civil and cultural movements between Korea and Europe. The Renaissance had a great impact on the birth of modern art, literature, philosophy, politics, and science. Renaissance scholars employed the humanist method in study, and searched for realism and human emotion in their endeavors.

The Renaissance was the transition from a middle-age era with its emphasis on god to modern history with its focus on people. Ko's "Airong" view derived from an early historical event at the beginning of Joseon Dynasty. When the dynasty founder, Yi Seong-gye revolted against the Goryeo Dynasty and successfully established his new regime, some of the

Goryeo loyalists were against the Yi's revolt. These Goryeo loyalists gave up their government service and stayed away from any active public role. Their attitude as a way of their protest was to ignore what was going around them. This attitude became a central theme of "Airong."

The literal interpretation of "Airong" is as follow: In Chinese characters, "A" means aphonia. "Irong" is for hard of hearing. Airong's origin was from Kim Ji-yeon's books, *Joseon* published in 1930 and *Joseon Folksong, Arirang* published in 1935. The Airong theory of Ko may have arisen from the hardship of Korean people during reconstruction of Gyeongbokgung Palace in the late 1867. Both the historical and the social environment explain the satire and resistance of the Korean people. Thus, Ko's Airong shows how the Korean people handled such a crisis. The emergence of the Airong

Gyeongbokgung Palace Geunjeongjeon

philosophy in Korea resembles that of Renaissance in Europe.

Airong's philosophy is also similar to that of non-violence resistance used by Mahatma Gandhi and Martin Luther King Jr. Ko Kwon-sam also suggests that Airong has its own uniqueness compared to Gandhi's non-violent resistance in India. Specifically, Airong philosophy had a great impact both on the non-violent movements and on Korean culture. His Airong theory further stresses the critical role of peace in the appreciation of culture and happiness. Thus, he claimes that Koreans are the leader of world peace.

In this regard, Ko concludes that the Airong philosophy is more aggressive and progressive than Gandhi's non-violent resistance which focused on resistance against oppressors. In summary, Arirang has been Koreans' spirit against the hardships that Koreans had to face. The two major hardships are the reconstruction of Gyeongbokgung Palace in the late 1867 and Japanese occupation from 1910 to 1945. In addition, Koreans have been experiencing the separation of Korea between South and North since 1945. Arirang encompasses all this historical and cultural aspects of Koreans' experiences. Therefore, Arirang carries more than musical and cultural value.

f. Yi Saek's Notion

Recently, some Arirang specialists disclosed their views regarding the origin of the song of Arirang. During the Goryeo to the Joseon periods, a distinguished scholar named Yi Saek wrote about the Chinese poets. In his work, he paid attention to the word 'Sheizhi(誰知)' Sheizhi means "Who knows? Who would have thought…?" This expression meaning "Who knows my heart, our hearts, or thinking?" was translated into Korean "Nuga Alliyo" and later it became Ariyo, Arariyo. As we've seen, Arirang has endless origins proposed. Some of them have similarities; however it is difficult to pick one conclusion. One common thing is that all the theories point to a Korean national emotion as embodied in Arirang. Regarding the origin, we may go back to the Silla, the Goryeo and the Joseon.

Regarding the geographical location, the music of Korea was influenced by China and the countries bordering on the Western Regions of China. Where did Arirang come from? Who sang the song for the first time? They might have sung the Arirang since Dangun founded the Korean nation about 4300 years ago. It might have been sung in Goguryeo, Silla and Baekje about 1500 years ago. Many scholars made arguments to find the origin and the original term of Arirang. In spite of this, they couldn't find out the clear origin and the original term of the song of Arirang.

One thing is certain: the song of Arirang was sung by the Korean people and in the Korean language. Lee Geun-bae, poet, clearly and simply states the origin and term of Arirang as follows: The song of Arirang was sung from long ago by the Korean people. It will continue forever as long as the Korean people exist.

4. The History of the Song of Arirang

On the origin of the song of Arirang, we examined the various views ranging from the Silla to the Modern period, Joseon. Those views were examined by the noted scholars, even though we cannot obtain the formative conclusion of the origin of the Arirang.

Under this circumstance, lately we may focus on two leading views: one is the ancient theory based upon the Silla, and the other is the modern theory based upon the Joseon in conjunction with the reconstruction of the Gyeongbokgung Palace by Daewongun.

I assume the modern theory has a more persuasive view rather than the ancient theory. But the discussion on its origin is continuing.

5. When was the Song of Arirang Named as Arirang?

The song of Arirang has been loved for a long time by Koreans and the people of the world as well. It has been sung since quite long ago, but it first appeared in the record in the late Joseon. The song of Arirang appeared in "Nongbusa" in *Mancheonyugo* (1790) written by Yi Seung-hun. He frequently went to China and was baptized as the first Christian in Korea. He was in jail due to his religion. He was a brother-in-law of Jeong Yak-yong, a famous scholar.

He wrote that the chorus of the song of Arirang was 'Arorong-Arorong-Eohiya.' Many believe that this is the earliest record on Arirang. They are not sure that it is the old version of the song of Arirang. But it does seem quite similar to the song of Arirang today. They did not know how it was actually sung.

The song of Arirang is found in the music scores recorded in the 19th century by foreigners like H. B. Hulbert. The song of Arirang was spreaded nationwide by the restoration of the Gyeongbokgung Palace.

Kim So-un, who introduced Korean folksong to Japan, noted that the song of Arirang is not an ancient song. He wrote that it was born during the restoration of the Gyeongbokgung Palace.

Takahashi Tohoru studied Korean philosophy and taught Korean language at Gyeongseong Imperial University(now Seoul National University) in Seoul during the Japanese occupation period. Takahashi thought the people were mobilized for the restoration of the Gyeongbokgung Palace from every corner of Korea. While working, they sang the folksong of their hometowns. Takahashi guessed that the construction site might have been something like a 'Folksong Fair of Korea.' The folksong were mixed and changed there.

Kim Yeol-gyu, former Professor at Sogang University and Kim Yeon-gap, the executive director of Korea Arirang Association, think that the song of Arirang was formed during the restoration of the Gyeongbokgung Palace. The song of Arirang has changed a lot over the years. It is a living song with great strength. That makes the song of Arirang outstanding among many folksong.

Many foreign scholars opinion that the song of Arirang is not very old. The majority of Korean scholars agree with them. They think the song of Arirang is about 100 years old.

Kim Tae-jun, who studied Korean folksong during the Japanese occupation period, wrote that the song of Arirang had a fixed form after the restoration of Gyeongbokgung

Palace. He pointed out that in the article "Introduction to Folksong of Joseon."

Tanabe Hisao, who contributed to the conservation of Korean royal court music also wrote that the song of Arirang was created through the restoration of Gyeongbokgung Palace. It is widely accepted that the song of Arirang did not appear in any record before the 19th century.

According to Kim Gi-hyeon, Professor of Kyungpook National University, both the scarcity of the record and the various names referring to the song of Arirang mean that the song of Arirang is a relatively new song born in modern times. He also said that the term 'Arirang' was used from 1921 and that the chorus "Arirang, Arirang, Arariyo… I am crossing over Arirang Pass" first appeared in the film *Arirang* directed by Na Un-gyu in 1926.

The oldest record about the song of Arirang appears in Yi Seung-hun's *Mancheonyugo*. And Hwang Hyeon wrote people sang "Arirang taryeong(meaning a tune)" in his book *Maecheonyarok*(1894). H. B. Hulbert recorded the "Ararung" in February 1896. Lee Sang-jun recorded the verses and the music score of Areurung taryeong in his book *Joseon Sokgokjip Part I*(1914).

Hulbert's 'Ararung' and Lee's 'Areurung taryeong' have similar verses, tunes and music scores in spite of an 18-year gap. Lee Sang-jun is from Jaeryeong, Hwanghae-do Province. He came to Seoul at the age of 12 and studied music in the

Pearson Bible Institute. He taught music in Daeseong School in Pyongyang, which was founded by Ahn Chang-ho.

After that, he recorded Korean folksongs on music paper working in Joseon Jeongak School. He also edited *Sinseongokjip* (1921, first edition; 1923, second edition) that contained Arirang and Gangwon-do Arirang. The difference from his former work *Joseon Sokgokjip Part I*(1914) is that the name changed from Areurung taryeong to Arirang. Based on those records, it can be concluded that the song of Arirang gained its stable name and form around 1921.

The restoration of Gyeongbokgung Palace began in 1865 and ended in 1867. It is nearly impossible for a song to be created and known well to common people in seven years. Before the reconstruction began, people sang songs like Ararang and Arongga in some areas. The songs were mixed and influenced one another when the reconstruction laborers worked together and sang together. As a result, Arirang was born. As to the diffusion, professional singers, the 'gisaeng', and wandering entertainers sang Arirang and other folksong as well(Kusano Taeko).

To summarize, the song of Arirang did not have a stable name or distinctive form until the mid-1920's. Arirang gained its reputation as a relatively new song around that time. The song of Arirang was finally born in the early 20th century. Even if we admit that the very beginning of the song of Arirang dates back to the Silla or the Gojoseon period like some people say, the song of Arirang obtained its name and form as it is today in the 20th century. Takahashi Tohoru also said that the song of Arirang emerged after the restoration of Gyeongbokgung Palace.

Meanwhile, Lee Gwang-su used the term 'Areurang' in his book *The Folksong No. 1* (1924). However, in 1930, he used the term 'Arirang' in his book *Who created the song of Arirang?* (1930). The song of Arirang was sung before the Japanese occupation began. One year after the occupation began, the Government General of Joseon (GGJ) collected folk speech and popular books of Joseon. The song of Arirang was included. Wada Tenmin also, recorded Arirang in his book *The Flavor of Joseon* (1920). Due to the lack of record, the ancient theory saying that the song of Arirang was created in the Silla Kingdom or the Gojoseon period seems less persuasive than the modern theory. I suspect that the modern theory is supported by a richer record and proof. To conclude, the song of Arirang is thought to have obtained its name after the restoration of Gyeongbokgung Palace.

The Story of Han and Arirang

The Sugam Valley fully covered with a Royal Azalea blossom(Jeongseon)

4

Chapter

1. The meaning of Han

The Korean word "Han" describes many different states of emotion in Korean culture. The literal meaning of "Han" is the feeling of everlasting, painful sorrow caused by betrayed love or social injustice. For Koreans, however, the true meaning of the word "Han" transcends this literal definition. I believe stories associated with Arirang may make clear the true meaning of "Han." Throughout history, Koreans have used Arirang to overcome life's hardships. During such times, many Koreans have used the song as a source of spiritual strength.

Let me start with the stories of Koreans who have used Arirang during difficult times. As I have discussed before, many Koreans endured indescribable hardship during the Japanese occupation of the 1940's. These unfortunate Korean People such as comfort women, forced laborers, conscripted soldiers and independent activists, were treated badly by the Japanese government during the war. Many of them perished at the war front. Throughout these times, it is reported that

Arirang was a source of spiritual strength.

Another well-known, tragic tale in Korean culture is the story of Crown Prince Sado. Crown Prince Sado(1735-1762) died after being imprisoned inside a large rice chest for eight days. His father, King Yeongjo, had ordered his execution based on advice from government officials who had heard unreliable rumors regarding Sado's mental health.

After Crown Prince Sado died, the Joseon honored him by naming him King Jangjo even though he never took the throne; however, the tragic circumstances surrounding his death tormented his wife, Queen Heongyeong, for the rest of her life. This true story represents one of the saddest events that occurred in the Joseon. Indeed, Koreans understand "Han" through Queen Heongyeong's sorrow.

Another Korean folk story that eloquently illustrates the meaning of "Han" is Chunhyang. This story describes the love between Chunhyang, the daughter of a 'gisaeng' (a member of the professional entertainers), and Yi Mong-ryong, the son of a magistrate. After the two got married in secret, Mong-ryong had to leave Chunhyang behind while taking the gwageo(highest state examination) in Seoul. After he went to Seoul with his family a new magistrate was appointed.

He, a bad-tempered and corrupt official, attempted to force Chunhyang to be his concubine. As she refused his order, the local magistrate tortured her and sentenced her to death. At the last minute, however, she was rescued by her husband, who had returned to his hometown as a secret royal inspector.

The agony and despair that Chunhyang had experienced at the hands of the corrupt magistrate is sharply contrasted with her elation when her husband returns to rescue her. Indeed, the story of Chunhyang epitomizes the complex combination of sorrow and happiness that defines "Han."

2. Han and Arirang

An example from modern Korean history (1900-present) is the oppression many Koreans experienced during the Japanese occupation. At that time many Koreans had their lands confiscated and were forced to leave their homeland for other countries such as Japan, China, Russia or America. These Koreans experienced the "Han" that I described earlier. An massive Korean immigration in 1980's to Europe, South America, and the US has brought the spirit of Arirang to other parts of the world as well. Arirang has been with these Koreans as they suffered through hardships and achieved success.

The true meaning of "Han" is the intertwined feeling of hardship and success. Indeed, Koreans found a sense of perseverance and open mindedness in the spirit of Arirang. This dual representation of Arirang has become a Korean symbol, characterizing the hope for Korea's future. I would like to revisit crucial facts revealing the spirit of Arirang and Han. First, Kim San's story about Arirang represents how many Koreans felt about their lives under Japanese occupation. He described Korea's hardship as follows: "It is a song of death in the end. It is a song of death and not of life. But death is not a defeat. Out of many deaths, victory may be born."

Although Arirang is often associated with times of sorrow, many Koreans also have a positive view on Arirang. Recently, many Koreans have considered Arirang to be a happy song. Again, one can clearly see that Koreans use Arirang to overcome emotional hardship in the past, present and future. Indeed, Arirang has provided a sense of positive emotional support for Koreans throughout history, in both times of sorrow and times of happiness.

Han has multiple connotations that describe deep emotions. Cheon Yi-doo recently explained Han using several different definitions. These include :

① a deep sorrow after giving up hope

② a unique inner beauty of Koreans

③ an inner feeling experienced by Koreans during a deeply-rooted emotional exercise

④ an experience and expression of Korean injustice and agony based upon reality, history and social interaction

⑤ a feeling associated with an unfulfilled hope, desire, or dream that still provides a lesson for a better future

Having lived outside Korea for over 40 years, I have come to appreciate the many differences between Korea and other countries. After completing my studies on Arirang, I found that the Han is a complicated expression of emotions that is very unique to

Koreans. It is my personal wish that people will appreciate the significance of Han in Korean culture by reading this book.

Here is my understanding of the notion of Han. First, Han is not the outcome of a rapid emotional outburst. Instead, Han is established gradually over several decades. For example, before the Joseon was established, many subjects of the previous regime did not approve of the revolt led by Yi Seong-gye. As such, they retired from public service and expressed their disapproval of the new regime until their death. These loyal subjects sacrificed their wealth and well-being to remain true to their principles and developed Han for the remainder of their lives.

Second, many Koreans do not openly show disappointment or sorrow. Often, these repressed feelings of sorrow and anger are transformed into the feeling of Han. These repressed emotions are often expressed in different versions of Arirang, such as Jeongseon Arirang. Undoubtedly, Han of many Koreans are associated with agony and happiness. Indeed, one Korean writer interpreted that Koreans resolve their Han through forgiveness. I find that Koreans are often able to use different versions of Arirang to express their Han. Indeed, Koreans have used the song as peaceful way of resolving their Han. Singing folksongs such as Arirang allows them to express their inner feelings of Han, thus giving them a way to move forward in their lives. I hope that the understanding Han will make the song of Arirang more meaningful.

The Film Arirang

The wild flowers at Mt. Hambaeksan(Jeongseon)

5

Chapter

1. Filmmaker and Actor Na Un-gyu

In 1925 the Korean film *SimCheongJeon* was produced by the director Lee Gyeong-seon . An actor Na Un-gyu played the main character of the film, the blind father, and he attracted public attention with the role.

One day, Na asked the director Lee for a material for a film script. Na wanted to produce a film for himself. In those days, director Lee was famous for a prodigy of writing screenplays while managing a group of performers. Director Lee gave an unfinished work to Na. The unfinished work included some poems, essays, and folksongs. A few days later Na read them all in a short time and one of the poems left a deep impression on Na's mind.

Finally, the film Arirang was created through the note given by the director Lee. Na had help from Tsumori Shuichi who was the director of production at Joseon Kinema to make the film. Everything went smoothly.

2. Production of the Film

This is the Cast:

Hero (Choi Yeong-jin): Na Un-gyu
Heroin, Yeong-jin's sister (Choi Yeong-hee): Shin Il-seon
Hero's friend (Yun Hyeon-gu): Un Nam-kung
Japanese police officer (Oh Gi-ho): Ju In-gyu

A Synopsis of the film Arirang is as following:

In a town, Yeong-jin is a madman living with his father and his younger sister Yeong-hee. One day, Yeong-jin's friend Hyeon-gu comes to visit and becomes heartbroken at Yeong-jin's sorrowful state. He meets Yeong-hee there and the two fall in love. Meanwhile, Oh Gi-ho, the household manager of the town's evil landlord, has feelings for Yeong-hee and tries to rape her on a town festival night when all the other townspeople are gathered up in the plaza. Hyeon-gu appears just in time and the two start fighting. Oh Gi-ho is hit by the sickle wielded by Yeong-jin and

Filmmaker and Actor Na Un-gyu

shocked at the sight of blood, Yeong-jin regains his sanity but he has already killed Oh Gi-ho. Yeong-jin is handcuffed by Japanese police officers and dragged off beyond the hills of Arirang Mountain.

(from Korea Film Database : http://www.kmdb.or.kr/eng/md_
basic.asp?nation=K&p_dataid=00033&searchText=arirang)

Na started shooting the film at Seoul in April 1926. Most of actors and actresses worked without being paid due to insufficient funds, except the heroin, Shin. On the climax scene of the film, about 500 extras were needed to complete the scene of a harvesting festival.

However, it was difficult to finish the task because it was

very cold at the time. Who would play in freezing cold? Na served 'makgeolli' (unstrained rice wine) to the extra players to help keep them warm. According to the passed anecdote, the drunken actors made a scene of carnage. They just danced and sang under the influence of liquor. Some just went off into a vinous sleep. With these happenings, Na was able to create more realistic scene.

Unfortunately, we are unable to access to this film anymore since the film is disappeared through the Japanese colinial period and Korean War. However, after 1926, Arirang have been produced repeatedly for various forms of popular culture such as film, play, opera, novel, popular song, so on. This demonstrates that Arirang have marked a truly important position for a popular culture not only of Korea but also of the World.

3. Censorship by GGJ

After Na finished editing the film *Arirang*, there was an obstacle to the release of the film. In 1926, GGJ began a so-called cultural administration to control Koreans' spirit. The GGJ put censorship on every publication and film from August 1, 1926. Fortunately, Na had made the acquaintance of Tsumori Shuichi, a Japanese. Na asked Tsumori to help him pass the censorship. When they filed for censorship, they wrote that the film Arirang was written and directed by Tsumori, a Japanese national. The GGJ passed the film Arirang, because they did not think it was against Japan.

Then, Na thought that everything was going be fine. However, the film flier was confiscated because the song of Arirang was on the flier. The GGJ thought some parts of the song of Arirang might stir resistance against GGJ. Finally, Na eliminated the problematic part from the flier. Ironically, this made the Korean people wonder about the film and long for the film more than ever.

4. The Best Box-Office Record

The film *Arirang* was a box-office hit and maintained its popularity almost for two years all over the country. There were two primary factors for the film's success. First, the film *Arirang* involved Korean people oppressed by Japanese occupation.

The film stood firmly for the weak and surpresed. Now that the film *Arirang* had spread out nationally and had a strong hold on the Korean public, the GGJ kept Koreans from singing the song of Arirang.

However, the more harshly the film and the song of Arirang were prohibited, the more eagerly Korean people watched and sang. The film won the ultimate popularity. The film *Arirang* spread the song of Arirang to the whole country.

5. Arirang in the Film *Arirang*

The song of Arirang was the main title of the film *Arirang*. Which is directed by Na Un-gyu. The song could be heard frequently. For instance, when Hyeon-gu dated Yeong-hee, he played Arirang with the violin for his lover. In this scene, the song of Arirang became the serenade of love.

When Yeong-jin listened to the melody of Arirang, he could sing the song of Arirang even though he had a serious mental breakdown. He could not communicate with his family, friends, or neighbors, but he did come out from his inner world when he heard the song of Arirang. At this time, the song of Arirang aroused the spirit from sleep. In addition, on the climax of the film, when Gi-ho tried raping Yeong-hee, her brother Yeong-jin stabbed him to death and then he came to himself.

The Japanese police took him to the police station on suspicion of murder. During this moment the song of Arirang played as background music. This Arirang was an anti-Japan symbol. Yeong-jin was taken to the police office with Korean

From left to right Na Un-gyu(Director), Kang Hong-shik(Leading actor), Lee Phil-woo (Recording), Choi In-kyu, before Cinematizing Hwangmooji(wilderness) courtesy called at Chosun Ilbosa(July 29, 1937).

neighbors watching. And the neighbors cried for him with the song of Arirang being played. In this scene Arirang was a song for miserable people who lost their country and suffered unfair treatment by the GGJ. The song of Arirang played many different roles from a love serenade to the national resistance theme. The reason why the film *Arirang* is so highly appreciated is that the film linked the folksong of Arirang with anti-Japan sentiment. Thus the film was not only entertaining but also enlightening.

Arirang's influence over the Korean people is unquestionable.

Dansungsa Theater :
past and present at Jongno(1)

Dansungsa Theater : past and present at
Jongno(2)

Dansungsa Theater : past and present at
Jongno(3)

There are countless folksongs in Korea. Then, why did Na pick the song of Arirang for the film? How did the song lead the whole mood and the story? The assumption is that the folksong Arirang is more than a song which has both at artistic effect and expresses the soul of the nation.

I would like to examine the role of Arirang from the film Arirang in Korean movements throughout Korea history.

When Goryeo collapsed, the loyal retainers sang the song of Arirang in Jeongseon to show they would not serve another regime, specifically the Joseon. Also under Japanese occupation, Arirang was sung by the Korean soldiers for national independence and had a significant role in the independence of Korea.

Arirang was also arranged to publicly announce the nationwide small-pox vaccination. Its title was Vaccination Arirang. Hangeul(Korean alphabet) Arirang was used for a campaign to eradicate illiteracy. In addition, the song of Arirang became popular as a theme of art. The Arirang is admittedly beautiful music for a film theme song, and many popular musicians arrange the Arirang in various ways to combine the traditional song with contemporary music. Thus, the Arirang is born again and again.

The Major Types of Arirang

The crater lake on the Mt. Baekdusan

6
hapter

There are quite a few types of Arirang. Let us list four major Arirang in South Korea. These include Seoul Arirang(Bonjo Arirang) in Gyeonggi-do Province; Jeongseon Arirang, Hanobaengnyeon, and Gangwon-do Arirang in Gangwon-do Province; Miryang Arirang in Gyeongsang-do Province; and Jindo Arirang in Jeolla-do Province. Those folksongs have different melodies by region.

However, those folksongs show similar emotion of the common people. Seoul Arirang and Jindo Arirang exhibit subtle moods which create sorrow. Jeongseon Arirang, Gangwon-do Arirang, and Hanobaengnyeon have the most sorrowful tone in South Korea. Of course, the song of Arirang is mostly characterized by sorrowful melodies. But Jeongseon Arirang defeats all. We may say that the sorrowful emotion of Jeongseon Arirang fully expresses the hearts of Koreans. Miryang Arirang has an up-and-down tune that is noted for its light rhythmical melody. These local Arirang are different from one another; they are alike in handling and overcoming Han(grudge).

1. Seoul/Gyeonggi Arirang

Korean

아리랑 아리랑 아라리요

아리랑 고개로 넘어간다

나를 버리고 가시는 님은

십리도 못 가서 발병난다

Romanization

A ri rang A ri rang A ra ri yo

A ri rang go gae ro neom eo gan da

Na reul beo ri go ga si neun nim eun

Sim ni do mot ga seo bal byeong nan da

English

Arirang Arirang Arariyo

I am going over the Arirang Hill(Pass)

He who leaves me, with me behind,

Will have trouble with his feet in no for distance

Korean

청천 하늘엔 별도 많고
우리네 살림살인 말도 많다

아리랑 고개로 열두 고개
구름도 사람도 쉬어간다

저기 저 산이 백두산 이야기
동지섣달에도 꽃만 핀다

a. The Official Song for the Unified Korea Team

Generally, Gyeonggi or Seoul Arirang is also called "Bonjo Arirang." Gyeonggi Arirang was Joseon as the official song for the Unified Korea Sports Team in 1990. But North Korea disagreed that the official song should be called Gyeonggi Arirang because Gyeonggi is a region which belongs only to South Korea. In the end, South Korea agreed with North Korea because both Korean residents abroad and foreigners have called the melody Arirang, not Gyeonggi Arirang. So the song, which was once called Gyeonggi Arirang, came to be called just Arirang.

b. Finding Gyeonggi Arirang

What is the real Seoul or Gyeonggi Arirang? Before the liberation in 1945, Seoul was a part of Gyeonggi-do. In other words, there must have been an Arirang which is unique to

Seoul /Gyeonggi Arirang

Nomal Speed, Softly

Chorus ♩ = 96-104

A ri rang＿ a ri rang＿ a ra＿ ri＿ yo＿

A ri rang＿ go＿ gae＿ ro＿ neo meo＿ gan da
Over the Arirang Hill I am going

Solo

Na reul beo＿ ri＿ go＿ ga sin eun ni＿ meun＿
He who leaves me, with me behind,

Sim ni do＿ mot＿ ga＿ seo＿ bal byeong nan da
Will have trouble with his feet in no for distance

Chorus

A ri rang＿ a ri rang＿ a ra＿ ri＿ yo＿

A - ri - rang＿ go - gae - ro＿ neo meo＿ gan da

Gyeonggi-do region. Seoul is the capital of Korea. Therefore, if there was Seoul Arirang, it would be the representative Arirang of Korea. There are a few evidences that an Arirang was sung in Gyeonggi-do region. Even though the author and the record of date were not accurate, we can find 'Arorong' in *Mancheonyugo* by Yi Seung-hun which is similar to Arirang. And *Maecheonyarok* which is about politicians in the 1860s gives a hint that the king and the queen of Joseon enjoyed Arirang.

Accordingly, it seems to be true that Arirang was already sung in Gyeonggi-do region. Unfortunately, as these documents contain neither the text nor the melody of the song, it cannot be recreated. In place of this, we can try to look into the previous source, the film sound track Arirang recorded in the 1920's. It might help.

Other than that, a musical score for 'Ararung' appeared in *Joseon yugi* (1896). An American missionary H. B. Hulbert recorded this. Even though this was recorded in two quarter measure, which is wrong, by a westerner, this is the oldest record about Arirang of the Gyeonggi-do region.

According to the documents, Arirang was 'Ararung' and the refrain was 'ol-sa pae tteui o ra.' The melody and the text are different from those of today. Besides, both *Hanbando* published in 1901 and H. N. Allen's *Things Korean* published in 1908 quoted the Arirang of H. B. Hulbert's version.

Another one is *Joseon Sokgokjip Part I* published in 1914.

This documentary was published by Lee Sang-jun who was one of forerunners of Western Music in Korea. The book is a breakthrough in westernization of Korean music. This was the first commercial book on music in Korea. What is important is that the score and article are equal to the documentary of H. B. Hulbert.

The rest of the works were *Sinchan Sokgokjip* published in 1921, and the volume two of *Joseon Sokgokjip* published in 1929. It can be concluded that the musical score is accurate as the musical score from many documents are identical. This was the score made by H. B. Hulbert in 1896.

Generally, the researchers tell Gyeonggi Arirang from Seoul Arirang(which they sometimes call "original Arirang"), however, I see two different Arirang as one Arirang because there is little difference between the two Arirang. And few evidence support that Seoul Arirang is the original one. Therefore, I use the term "Gyeonggi Arirang" to mean Seoul Arirang and Gyeonggi Arirang together because Seoul is located in the middle of Gyeonggi-do Province.

c. Features of Gyeonggi Arirang

The original role of Gyeonggi Arirang seems to have the 'role of carrier' as Jungwon Arirang. The canal connecting Gangwon-do Province and the Seoul area could be called the 'road of Arirang,' when the Gyeongbokgung Palace was being reconstructed by Daewongun; people who worked on timber-carrying boats would pass the song of Arirang such as 'Unified Eight Province Songs.'

However, this is not very clear in terms of cultural perspective. We can assume that the origin of Gyeonggi and Jungwon Arirang began for geographical reason, and the film *Arirang* made Arirang a nationally popular song. The Gyeonggi Arirang seems to have started among ordinary people around the 18th century and developed with historic incidents. It also seems to be affected by miscellaneous songs of Gyeonggi and Gangwon-do Arirang. Hence, Gyeonggi Arirang had an important role related to the origin of Jindo, Miryang, Haeju, Anseong, Yeongcheon, and Daegu Arirang.

2. Jeongseon Arirang

Korean

눈이 올라나 비가 올라나 억수장마 질라나

만수산 검은 구름이 막 모여든다

아우라지 뱃사공아 배 좀 건네주게

싸리꼴 올동박이 다 떨어진다

아리랑 아리랑 아라리요

아리랑 고개고개로 나를 넘겨주게

Romanization

Nun i ol la na bi ga ol la na eok su jang ma jil la na

Man su san geom eun gu reum i mak moyeo deun da

A u ra ji baet sa gong a bae jom geon ne ju ge

Ssa ri gol ol dong bak i da tteo reo jin da

A ri rang a ri rang a ra ri yo

A ri rang go gae go gae ro na reul neom gyeo ju ge

English

Will it snow, will it rain or pour for the season?
Dark clouds are swarming from above Mt. Mansusan
Oh Ferryman of Auraji, take me over the river
Blossome of oldongbak in Ssarigol are falling down
Arirang arirang arariyo.
Pass me over the Arirang Hill.

Korean

정선 같은 살기 좋은 곳 놀러 한 번 오세요
검은 산 물밑이라도 해당화가 핍니다

맨드라미 줄봉숭아는 토담이 붉어 좋구요
앞 남산 철쭉꽃은 강산이 붉어 좋다

앞 강에 흐르는 물은 막을 수나 있지만
가는 세월 지는 해는 막을 수 없네

a. The Road to Jeongseon Arirang

I visited Korea again in 2005 in order to visit Jeongseon which is one of four hometowns of major Arirang in South Korea. I have never visited this place before. I never even dreamed that I could visit this place. I was so excited to visit this place because I was guided by experts of the field of Arirang; Kim Yeon-gap and Ki Mi-yang. I also felt a little bit scared due to the heavy traffic leading to Jeongseon. However,

Jeongseon is slowly running around by the Joyanggang River

the view of jeongseon was so beautiful that I was very happy.

The Joyanggang River was slowly running around this town and the scenery was stunning. Across the river, there is Mt. Bibongsan; the view was a master piece of picture and the sky was so blue and clear. I found the memorial stone of Arirang; the expert guide explained the origin of the stone and the meaning of the inscription on the stone. It says that "Originally it was called 'Arari' but it became the popular Arirang; the lyric implies, "who should understand me and the circumstances surrounding me?" This is originally 'who should know my burning mind. Please understand me.' Arirang has been changed like Ali ("Who should know?" in

Jeongseon Arirang

Sorrowfully

Nun i ol la na bi _ ga ___ ol la ___ na ___
Will it snow, will it rain

eok su jang ma ___ jil la ___ na ___
or pour for the season?

Man _ su ___ san geom eun ___ gu reum ___ i ___
Dark clouds are swarming

mak mo yeo ___ deun ___ da ___
from above Mt. Mansusan.

A u ra ji ___ baet sa gong ___ a ___
Oh Ferryman of Auraji,

bae jom geon ne ___ ju ___ ge ___
take me over the river.

Korean)→Arari→Arirang. According to the recent research, 'Meari' (mountain echo) seems to be the origin of Arirang.

b. The Natural Environment and People of Jeongseon

Jeongseon is located in a valley and is a part of the east of the Korean Peninsula. So this place is famous for the deep forest and recreational resort. Jeongseon area consists of 80% of forest and 20% agricultural land where sweet corns, potatoes and beans are raised. The Arirang developed from grief, sadness, happiness and love. Jeongseon people used their hardships of daily life as a source of Arirang melody. It made them feel better during hard agricultural work and the joyful melody made them happy. It has a catharsis function which mitigates people's grief, sickness of daily life, and hard married lives especially of women. Arirang melody also was a nursery song.

The number of different versions of Jeongseon Arirang exceeds 7,000 over the years and the various word show different colors of emotions. Therefore, Jeongseon people think that Arirang of other areas are fake Arirang because the songs do not contain their words. We can meet people who sing Arirang with their own words in Jeongseon, Pyeongchang and Yeongwol area. These Arirang songs created by individual Arirang singers are called "Arari." There is a feeling of blues in Jeongseon Arirang.

c. The Historical Background of Jeongseon

Jeongseon has been called *Taoyuan* which can be translated as paradise. Taoyuan has been mentioned in *Taoyuan Journey* written by Tao Yuanming. Taoyuan means the good place to live and the heaven on earth for people.

Jeongseon is located in the middle of Donghae and Samcheok, Taebaek and Pyeongchang, and Gangneung. The population is approximately 50,000 and the territory is about 1,220.63km². Basically there used to be only one village but now there are four different villages. Jeongseon has survived this environment. The humor and fun implied in Jeongseon Arirang makes people laugh and sometimes cry. The speech of Gangneung sounds softer and slower: it sounds innocent due to its unique characteristics.

d. The Formation of Jeongseon Arirang

Before we recap the Auraji fairy-tale, we have to become familiar with few words. "Auraji" means the merger of two water flows. "Jijanggu" is the name of a sailor who played janggu (hourglass-shaped drum) very well. There are some rocks on which the names of sailors are carved. Ssarigol is a village name. Oldongbak is a early blooming camellia which has a yellow blossom.

A lady and a bachelor fell in love with each other but there was a river flowing between two lovers. There was a person that they liked. He was the sailor who carried the lady or the bachelor across the river. His family name was "Ji." One day, it rained heavily, so no boat could go on the water. Two lovers were worried that they couldn't meet soon. The ferry man Ji could do nothing, either.

After that incident, ferryman Ji sang a song in memory of the lovers. Jeongseon people who got on the boat felt sorry for them listening to the song. Even now, there is a boat on the river, which does not run on water.

It is like a memorial monument. I wanted to step on this boat but I couldn't because of the absence of the sailor. On the other hand, a statue of the lady is standing on the shore of the river. In 1392, Yi Seong-gye who was a new emerging power in the late Goryeo killed Jeong Mong-ju who was the civil minister of Goryeo, and then he acceded to the throne by himself to establish the Joseon. Finally, the Goryeo collapsed. At that time, the seven great loyalists of Goryeo refused to serve the Joseon.

They kept the belief that a loyal retainer would not serve a second master. Thus, they were expelled out of the capital city and retired to their hermitage in the mountain of Jeongseon. Afterwards the expelled seven retainers lived in Jeongseon.

Today the town was named Geochilhyeondong in commemoration of their commitment. The sequestered life in Jeongseon was neither relaxing nor pleasant. The secluded loyalists always missed their former master, and their families. So they sang a song to appease the sorrow. Some say that the

A statue of lady stands at Auraji

song became Arirang and this was the origin of the Jeongseon Arari. Others think differently. They think the secluded retainers only recorded the songs of Jeongseon people for they were knowledgeable enough to record the songs with Chinese characters. They think that the birthplace of Jeongseon Arirang is the entire Jeongseon area, not Geochilhyeondong(Jin Yong-seon). To sum up, there are elements that have enriched Jeongseon Arirang. Jeongseon was a remote place with harsh living conditions; a place of exile during the Joseon Dynasty; a shelter when the Korean War broke out. The sorrow of the original Jeongseon people and that of those who came to Jeongseon for various reasons sing triggered them to songs of

The annual ceremony to worship Seven Wisemen, the fathers of Arirang

their own. The songs were mixed and evolved to become Jeongseon Arirang.

The melody of Jeongseon Arirang has the features of Gaeseong region, the vestige of the Goryeo court music. We can also find the influence of Buddhist music in it. According to Kim Gi-su, geographically or historically Jeongseon Arirang is related with chanting a sutra. The mood of reading a sutra is in adagio tempo. This is very similar to the mood of Jeongseon Arirang.

On the other hand, there is another story on the origin of Arirang. Once upon a time, a beautiful lady wished to marry a man who lived in Jeongseon. The groom was too young to marry. He was too immature to know what marriage is. The bride thought her husband did not love her, so she made up her mind to kill herself. One night, she went out to the river to die, and she saw the water wheel of a mill near the river. Suddenly an idea hit her. "Just like the waterwheel turning around ceaselessly, if I give him 3 months, he will become love me then." Then she decided to go back home and she sang Jeongseon Arirang on her way to home.

Let me introduce one more origin of Jeongseon Arirang. In the middle of 16th century a Purge of Confucian literati 'Eulsa sahwa' took place in the period(1545) of King Myeongjong's reign. At that time, many highly educated scholars and former bureaucrats exiled themselves from the capital and hid in rural areas. They looked back into the past singing the song of Arirang.

The most typical feature of Gangwon-do Province is its geological settings. The area is surrounded by mountains and enclosed by Taebaek Mountain Range. The isolated life in the devastated region caused suffering. Jeongseon Arirang reflected the sorrowful life. Tracing the origin of Jeongseon Arirang is the path to find the history of the territory.

e. The Inscription on Memorial Monument

A memorial monument stands on Mt. Bibongsan. The posture of this monument looks different from other memorial monuments: This monument is located on the middle of the mountain. It explains the history and the words of Jeongseon

Jeongseon Arirang Monument stands on Mt. Bibongsan

Arirang very well.

Here I would like to summarize Jeongseon Arirang for better understanding. The origin of Arirang was that seven surviving retainers of Goryeo secluded themselves from society at Geochilhyeondong, Jeongseon. They appeased the sorrow by composing and singing poems. It became the origin of Arirang. 1) The historical background relative to Korean's surviving retainers. 2) The cultural background relative to the place name of Geochilhyeondong. 3) Wearing a black suit every morning whether it may snow or rain. There are dark clouds in Mt. Mansusan…seem to lament over the national ruin. 4) Local Arirang in the whole country overlap with Jeongseon Arirang. These evidences prove that Arirang came from Jeongseon. While the origin of Arirang became steadfast as Jeongseon Arirang, the meaning of word was not firm yet. There are two reasons: Arirang was handed down by word of mouth and it was a song of the lower class.

f. The Characteristics of Jeongseon Arirang

Jeongseon Arirang has a typical tone of Gaeseong, the former capital of the Goryeo. It was also affected by the Buddhist music of the Goryeo which chanted virtuous deeds. Jeongseon Arirang touches the hearts of the listeners. The audience simultaneously feels mild and intense, and tight and free. This is the unique point of Jeongseon Arirang. Jeongseon Arirang creates the two contrary moods as if the blues with adagio tempo coincides with the chanting of the Buddhist scriptures.

In short, the distinctive feature is the free rhythm which often crosses over the boundary between the adagio and mosso tempo. The music of Mongolian 'Hoomii' has a similar feature. The contrary rhythms occur at the same time in the song of Hoomii. Bogino duu has the pattern of rhythm. On the other hand, Urtyn duu has no pattern of rhythm. So these two rhythms happen in one song. Professor Kusano identified the automatic rhythm and the contrary rhythm in one song.

Particularly, the terminology 'Jin' as of Jin song, Jin melody, Jin tempo, and Jin sound in Korean music means a long sound, which is 'Urtyn duu' in Mongolia.

The terms match as follows :

Nation	Non-rhythm	Rhythm
Korea	Jin	Jajin
Japan	Oiwakebushi	Yaskibusi
Mongolia	Urtyn duu	Bogino duu

(Kusano Taeko)

However, the Jin rhythm is rare in Korean folksong, and those songs were found in limited areas such as Hwanghae-do, Pyeongan-do, northern Gyeonggi-do, and Gangwon-do Provinces. The Jin rhythm is what you might call 'Oiwakebushi' in Japanese. According to Professor Kusano, one day a Japanese asked her, "Do Koreans have a song similar to Oiwakebushi? I have heard a song Hanobaengnyeon from Korea. The song sounds like just Oiwakebushi." The song of Hanobaengnyeon is one of the representative songs for Gangwon-do Province. Cho Yong-pil who is one of the most popular singers in Korea arranged and sang the song. He sang the song with affluent voice handling with automatic melody and driving the emotion of the audience.

As shown in the previous table, the similarity between the folksong of Japan and Korea is in the melody. This is why the

Korean song Hanobaengnyeon sounded familiar to the Japanese audience. Jeongseon Arirang has many connections to foreign countries. People say that Jeongseon Arirang is very similar to the Hoomii, Oiwakebushi, and Oharabushi.

For instance, late Kim Dae-jung who was the president of South Korea,visited Mongolia in May 1999. He said in the official address that "There is a particular relationship between Arirang and Mongolian music. Korea and Mongolia are the two countries able to sing Arirang.

Hoomii is a kind of singing with throat and is the traditional vocal technique in Mongolia. What is noteworthy about Hoomii is that the singer makes two different sounds simultaneously. With growling in his or her throat, he or she simultaneously makes a high-pitched tone. This technique is very rare in the world. People say that Hoomii is like a mysterious sound created by blowing wind in the vast open field. The clear high-pitched tone harmonizes with the low thick sound.

There are people who assume that Hoomii is linked to ancient religious practice and belief. With awe of powerful forces in the universe, it may have been used for meditation or for magical healing. People wonder how one person can physically produce such dual sounds. Musicologists and others have been carrying out a considerable amount of research on this over the last 10 years. Professional Hoomii performers are found in quite a few areas with certain traditions and unusual natural environments: the mountains, rivers and birds. They are mostly in the western part of Mongolia. Some say this sound was created while human beings imitated the sound of river and echo in the deep forest. Others say that this dawned with the sound of calling livestock. Hoomii prevails throughout the western Mongolia, and partially spreads out to Central Asia, which is known as Tuvin or the vicinity of Altai Mountain Range, 'Khalkh.' When people sing the Hoomii, they can use their noses, throats, chests, and abdomens to sing.

Thus, the singer needs to be strong to sing Hoomii. That is one of the reasons why singing Hoomii is a taboo for women. Hoomii is known to be hard to sing. Roughly one out of a thousand trained Mongolians can obtain the perfect technique. Therefore female singers are very rare. In addition, Hoomii is called a dark sound: it is a music of throat sound. Hoomii is designated as a Representative List of the Intangible Cultural Heritage of Humanity by UNESCO.

Jeongseon Arirang shows the lives of Jeongseon people of the past and the present. It is different from Jindo Arirang or Miryang Arirang in that the gap between highest and lowest pitch is not too big. The melodies are smooth and simple. Additionally, the melody is relatively short so that anyone can easily create his/her own lyrics to the Arirang melody. This is the reason why we call it "a user-created Arirang." Jeongseon Arirang is attached to the lives of Jeongseon people. Not only does it have a slow tempo of melody, but it also has a give and take game allowing different words depending on singers.

The 10 features of Jeongseon Arirang can be summarized as follows :

① Jeongseon Arirang has an emotional or melancholy blues of melody in which the words depict the hardship of human life.

② There was not only one melody or a set of lyrics but various lyrics which represent different times and backgrounds of Jeongseon people.

③ The lyrics show different emotions of people : There are no artificial emotions or manipulated representation.

④ There was a choir type of Arirang which was sung by Jeongseon people in order to lessen the burden of their agricultural life.

⑤ There are many types of the song of Arirang describing natural sublimes and human' s life.

⑥ More impromptu created lyrics are reported than lyrics written by official poets.

⑦ Some of the variations of the song of Arirang are composed of lyrics created by scholars.

⑧ There are also sexual appeals of lyrics created by local folks.

⑨ There is some evidence that Jeongseon people used Chinese characters.

⑩ There are many versions of Arirang melodies and lyrics which basically originated from Jeongseon Area.

g. The Farmers Market of Jeongseon in Every 5 days

Jeongseon is famous for not only the song of Arirang but also for various herbs. You can find almost every herb in the mountains of Jeongseon. Particularly, the indigenous herbs produced in Jeongseon are regarded as a tonic medicine. Gondeure (a kind of herb) is a most renowned herb in Jeongseon.

You can never sate yourself with the Gondeure because the leaf and the stalk are very soft and delicious. You can imagine the life of Jeongseon once you taste the Gondeure since the Gondeure grows wild only in Jeongseon area. Jeongseon has a lot of specialty food such as olchaengi noodle, kkotdeungchigi noodle, hwanggi pork hock, buckwheat snack, buckwheat pie, buckwheat soup and potato soup. Jeongseon is the sole place to taste those foods.

You can experience all of Jeongseon in the local market places. The local market is held every 5 days in any small town of Jeongseon. Also, in the local market, the rustics of Jeongseon open their own typical culture to the urbanites from out of Jeongseon. The market helps Jeongseon people communicate and exchange with the urbanites. The market is filled with yearning for the rural life of the urbanites. And the music cannot be omitted from this lively place. The Arari of

The Farmers Market of Jeongseon in Every 5 days

Jeongseon flows everywhere. The Arari with mosso temp excites the people to cheer on the moment.

h. Jeongseon Arirang Festival - Finding the Origin of Jeongseon Arari

Jeongseon Arari is the sound that helps people release grudge(Love/hate). The lyrics of Jeongseon Arari are based upon the sorrow of parting, the hard life, and the tearful love story. Jeongseon Arari survived a long time.

Finally the Jeongseon Arari was designated as Intangible Cultural Property No.1 of Gangwon-do in 1971. And the Jeongseon Arari has been identified as the origin of the whole

A participatory festival held for enhancement of community identity

Arirang.

Thus the Jeongseon-gun Office has held the Jeongseon Arari Festival since 1976, and this made the song known to the rest of Korea. Today the festival shows the song to the world. All attendants of the festival might try singing the Jeongseon Arari to feel the mood. And also they are able to experience some activities like Jeongseon Opera, learning the song of Arari, the traditional swinging, the traditional wrestling, and so on.

The festival is more for participating rather than sightseeing. After the festival, the attendants go back home to different cities, states, and even countries; they would sometimes recollect the festival by looking at photos. And also they would sing the song of Arari to themselves. This is the valuable outcome of the Jeongseon Festival.

i. Jeongseon *Ariranggeuk* (Korean Traditional Opera)

The visitors from all over the places watched the demonstration of Ariranggeuk Opera at Jeongseon Culture and Art Center located near Jeongseon market place. I was so excited to watch this. There was nothing special on stage: it just looked like a contemporary play but it made me recollect my childhood. Finally, the curtain is raised and an elderly woman was teaching Arirang to a little girl. However, this girl does not like to learn because she is too bored to keep learning. The girl falls asleep and she dreams that Seven Wisemen of the Goryeo are singing the song of Arirang, worrying about their endangered nation.

The main character "Jeongseon" sings a song which sounds very sad and elegant. The history gets started with this music. In act 2, it shows a scene of the Korean War (1950- 1953) with very great sound effects, so I did not even realize I was clapping my hands. Some people cried while watching very emotional scenes and others exclaimed at evoking scenes. It was a very emotional traditional opera for a man beside me who was crying, just like me.

Finally the little girl realizes and learns about the Korean War, a tragic event in Korean history. She resumes learning

The village of Jeongseon Arari

Jeongseon Arirang in act 3. The spring has come and all actors and actresses take the stage. They sing and dance. It is surprising that the opera is performed by all amateurs, elderly over 50 years, and ordinary people who work on the farm. They perform so wonderfully as they are singing about their own lives. There is purity and innocence, it is anything but artificial. It is a real Arari.

After Ariranggeuk Opera, I reflected that it contained the real soul and spirit of Koreans. We became stronger through hardships, challenges, and pains. We have loyalty and patriotism which will never fail. The song of Arirang has the local color. All Arirang from different places have their own

Jeongseon Ariranggeuk(Opera)

features. Jeongseon Arirang differs from Miryang Arirang and Jindo Arirang. Due to geographical factors, Jeongseon Arirang shows similarity to Japanese folksongs in terms of the musical scale, the musical interval, and the musical order. Some theory explains it as East Sea Cultural Circle or Japanese Cultural Circle. For instance, if a foreigner who speaks neither Korean nor Japanese listens to Gangwon-do folksong and Japanese folksong, he/she would think both songs are the same. The similarity between the mode of the Eastern Korean folksong and that of Japanese is amazing for those studying traditional music.

Professor Kusano indicated that studying the similarity

between the culture of the East Sea, Japan, and Korea is important. Furthermore, she alluded that Jeongseon Arirang has a close relationship with the Buddhist music of Mongolia. I am fully supportive of her statement, when the Pacific Science Conference was held in Seoul, Korea in 1986, I presented the paper entitled *The Vestiges of Korean migration in the Sanin and Hokuriku regions in ancient Japan*. In this paper, I clearly indicated the similarity between the ancient Japanese culture along the coast of the East Sea and the Korean culture. Research on the relationship between Japan and Korea in culture should be kept on.

3. Miryang Arirang

Korean

날좀 보소 날좀 보소 날좀 보소
동지섣달 꽃 본 듯이 날좀 보소
아리아리랑 스리스리랑 아라리가 났네
아리랑 고개로 날 넘겨주소

Romanization

Nal jom bo-so nal jom bo-so nal jom bo so
Dongji seot dal Kkot bon deu si nal jom bo so
A ri a rirang seu ri seu ri rang a ra ri ga nan ne
A ri rang- go gae ro nal neom gyeo ju so

English

Turn around to me, if once,
As if a flower in the freezing season
Ariarirang seuriseurirang ariganane
Pass me over the Arirang Hill.

Miryang Arirang

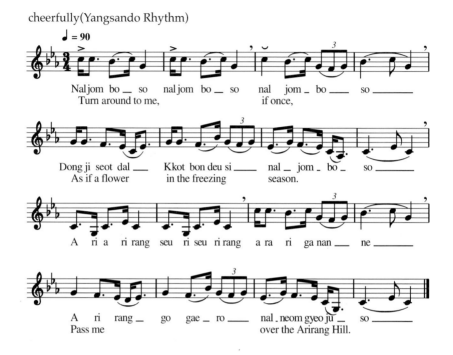

cheerfully(Yangsando Rhythm)

Nal jom bo _ so nal jom bo _ so nal jom bo ___ so ____
Turn around to me, if once,

Dong ji seot dal ___ Kkot bon deu si ____ nal _ jom _ bo _ so ____
As if a flower in the freezing season.

A ri a ri rang seu ri seu ri rang a ra ri ga nan ___ ne ____

A ri rang _ go gae _ ro ____ nal _ neom gyeo ju _ so ____
Pass me over the Arirang Hill.

Korean

정든 님 오시는데 인사를 못해

행주치마 입에 물고 입만 방긋

지척이 천리라더니 도랑 사인데

호박잎만 흔들흔들 날 속인다

Miryang Arirang is a typical folksong of Gyeongsang-do Province. Arirang is also sung in Seoul and all over the country. Being sung in Semachi Tune, it consists of 5 scales. Because of huge breadth between a soprano and an alto, we can feel the dynamics of the music. Therefore, this Arirang has often been arranged for martial, dancing, and ceremonial songs. There is folklore related to Arang who was a daughter of the Magistrate of Miryang and was killed by a servant. People began to sing a song "Arang Arang" in mourning for her death.

a. The Origin of Miryang Arirang : the Legend of Arang

Regarding the origin of Arirang, there are many theories. Among them, the legend of Arang is one of the most influential one. The following is the Legend of Arang :

Miryang in Gyeongsang-do Province is famous for the song of Miryang Arirang. The Arang's towered mansion is located near the railway close to Yeongnamnu Pavilion. The Arang's towered mansion is on the riverside and there is the tombstone and the graveyard of Arang. On every April 16, on the lunar calendar, they hold memorial services comforting the soul of Arang.

They say the name of Arang turned into Arirang, which is the name of the folksong, Miryang Arirang. Let me briefly summarize the origin of Arirang theory related to Miryang Arirang. Once upon a time in Miryang, there lived the Magistrate of Miryang whose wife passed away while giving birth to a daughter. The magistrate lived with his daughter

Miryang Arirang Monument

who he loved very much.

One day the daughter and her nurse went missing. Despite the search by all Miryang people, there was no trace. Thus, the magistrate finally lost his mind and resigned the job. He returned to Hanyang(now Seoul), the capital where he died in grief. After this incident, every new magistrate who came to Miryang was found dead on the very first morning. This is repeated a couple of times. Since then, no one applied for the position of magistrate of Miryang. Even though the central government tried hard to fill the post, it remained vacant for quite a long time.

A veteran officer learned about the situation. He had retired from military service 20 years before. For the past 20 years, he was unable to get a job. Thus he was in his sixties. His life was miserable because of being short of clothing to wear and food to eat. Clearly, he was having a hard time. To overcome this miserable life he tried to find a job to make a living.

One day he heard about the story of recruitment regarding the post of the magistrate. Then he discussed applying for the job with his wife. His wife said to him, "We know that any newly appointed magistrate passes away the next day. If you go there you may also lose your life. If you luckily survive it will be great. Even if you die, you die as a magistrate at least. Why not take the job? You should take it. I will go with you." This made him decide to apply for the job.

He was high-spirited. He immediately rushed to the central government office in order to apply for the post of Magistrate of Miryang. He said to the government officer, "I am not a capable man. I do not have any special talent, but I am an old veteran. If I get appointed, I will do my best. Please send me to Miryang."

Practically government authorities were suspicious about his ability. But there was no choice. Thus, they appointed him immediately, and the old soldier was the Magistrate of Miryang.

He returned home with some sort of worry. The old soldier told his wife, "Upon your suggestion and encouragement, I applied for the job then I obtained it. I might die the next day after we arrive in Miryang. However, I do not regret it. I am a magistrate even if I die. I think this is the best for me and my family." His wife responded, "It is unbelievable that the magistrates of Miryang were killed by the ghost. Even though I am a woman, I can escort you. Please do not worry about it. Just take me to Miryang with you."

The new magistrate left for Miryang with his wife. After they arrived at Miryang he took over the job. The local government officers came one after another to see him but they were not polite to the new boss. They actually paid no attention to him because they thought the new magistrate would also die in a day. He and his wife sensed that. Furthermore, seeing the magistrate escorted by a woman, his wife, the local government officers were disappointed. They went back to their office rooms grunting. The official residence for the magistrate was not tidy because the officers did not repair and clean it up. Furthermore, the janitors and office boys returned home before completing their job.

At last the fearful night was coming close. The wife asked her husband to stay in her room. "I will wear your official outfit and then I will go to the magistrate's office in order to find out what's going on there." She sat by herself in the office. Around midnight, suddenly a strange wind blew the candle light out. She felt a chill. In a moment the big gateway opened without noise. Then a woman smeared with blood and whose hair was disheveld came in holding a red flag. The wife of the magistrate did not move an inch.

"You might have a grudge toward someone and you have come in order to report it to the officer. I promise to handle your grudge for you. But you should wait for the time being. Please, you should not come again," the wife of the magistrate said gently. Then the ghost lady bowed and went out. The wife went to her room to tell her husband that the ghost had gone. "Now there is nothing to fear. Please wake up."

As the day dawned, there came a noisy crowd. They were the officers, the servant and the employees. They brought things for a funeral. They were arguing to decide who would go into the room. They thought that the magistrate should be dead. In fact, they had come to clean up the body of the magistrate. No one dared open the door. The magistrate came out of the office in full dress and told them in a loud voice "What are you doing? What are those you have in your hands?"

They could not believe their eyes. They were shocked to see the magistrate alive. They instantly respected him. The magistrate scolded them for being impolite to him and his wife the previous day and fired some of the corrupted officers. Also, the magistrate announced his administration policy and ordered that they should observe the rules and instructions he

Yeongnamnu Pavilion

would make.

The magistrate collected the information reported by his wife, who had a conversation with the ghost. The ghost was probably the daughter of the former magistrate who was known to be missing. He started the investigation secretly, and examined the list of stewards. After a close examination, he finally picked a suspect, Jugi. Shortly he called the officers to arrest Jugi and then put him on the rack to investigate. People gathered to see what was going on. The magistrate said, "You should know the former magistrate's daughter Arang. You must confess honestly." The voice was grave. Jugi was trembling with fear and his face was pale. Jugi confessed everything.

Notice board of Aranggak Shrine

The folks of the region came to see what he did to Arang. The nurse and Arang lived together in a house. Arang was fond of her nurse. Knowing this, Jugi who loved Arang secretly tried to pay off the nurse. He promised to give the nurse money if she took out Arang to the Yeongnamnu Pavilion where Arang and the nurse used to go out for a walk. The Yeongnamnu Pavilion is located in the back of the residence. The nurse was greedy for the money. She proposed that she and Arang go to appreciate the moon night together. While Arang was enjoying the lovely scene, the nurse disappeared. Then Jugi rushed to Arang and fetched her. Then he attempted to violate her.

Arang fiercely resisted. Knowing that he was unable to carry out his plan, he decided to keep the victim and the witness silent forever. If he was arrested, Jugi would be sentenced to death. Then he pulled out a knife and killed Arang and the nurse.

After the investigation, the magistrate reported to the central government. Then magistrate ordered to execute a death sentence for jugi. He also ordered to dig out the body of Arang. The clothes smeared with blood were put into a casket and sent to her father in Hanyang. Finally Arang was buried in her family graveyard.

Since then Miryang thrived day by day. The magistrate was respected by all. After he finished up his term, he returned to Hanyang. They lived happily thereafter. Miryang people assumed that the song of Arirang originated from the Legend of Arang.

b. Yeongcheon Arirang

In 2005, I had planned to go to Daegu and then to Yeongcheon in order to attend the Yeongcheon Arirang Festival. When we arrived at Yeongcheon, it was raining. Shortly after the arrival, we met Kim Dae-won. After having a lunch together, we went to the Yeongcheon Festival. The festival was held at a closed school. The school, which was rebuilt as a gallery looked very elegant and modern. I especially hope the Sian gallery will prosper, infusing Arirang

Yeongcheon Arirang Festival

in art works.

All the seats were taken before the festival started. Late comers were standing up in the back. Everyone put on a raincoat and clapped hands in joy. No one left their seats, and performers and staff acted unbelievably on the stage. The show included various perforances: modern dance, the orchestra performance, Yeongnam Arirang medley by Jeong Eun-ha and her pupil and activist singer An Chi-hwan. The performers and the audience were united as one. It compensated for the long and weary travel there. We all were very satisfied with the festival, especially with the quality of equipment and the professional performers.

Here are the lyrics of Yeongcheon Arirang and Gyeonggi

Arirang. According to an explanation, these two Arirang were sung by original Gyeonggi people who moved to China before liberation in 1945. After the liberation, the songs were sung widely in North Korea. These are known to South Korea since Kim Dae-jung visited North Korea in 2000. I was lucky to listen to the meaningful song in the hometown on the song, Yeongcheon.

There are many festivals in Yeongcheon such as 'Fruit Festival', 'Herb Medicine Festival', 'Bohyeonsan Starlight Festival', 'Science Festival' and 'Yeongcheon Art Fete.' I had hoped to attend all the listed festivals, because Arirang must be sung at each and the song would make each event more cheerful.

4. Jindo Arirang

Korean

아리아리랑 스리스리랑 아라리가 났네 헤 헤

아 아리랑 응응응 아라리가 났네

서산에 지는 해는 지고 싶어 지느냐

날 두고 가시는 님 가고 싶어 가느냐

Romanization

A ri a ri rang seu ri seu ri rang a ra ri ga nan ne he he

A a ri rang eung eung eung a ra ri ga nan ne

Seo san e ji neun hae neun ji go si peo ji neu nya

Nal du go ga si neun nim ga go si peo ga neu nya

English

Ariarirang seuriseurirang arariganannehehe

Aarirang eung eung eung ararigananne

Will the sun ever set for its won longing?

Will my love ever leave me for his own yearning?

Jindo Arirang

cheerfully(Yangsando Rhythm)

♩.=90

A ri a ri rang seu ri seu ri rang a ra ri ga nan ne ___ he _ he

A a ri rang eung eung eung a ra ri ga ___ nan ne ___

Seo san e ji neun hae neun ji go ___ si peo ji neu nya ___
Will the sun ever set for its won longing?

Nal du go ___ ga si neun nim ga go si peo ga neu nya
Will my love ever leave me for his own yearning?

Korean

문경새재는 웬 고갠가

굽이야 굽이야 굽이 가는 눈물이 난다

노다가세 노다가세

저 달이 떴다 지도록 노다가세

a. The Birthplace of Jindo Arirang

Jindo is one of the four birthplaces of Arirang. One crisp
and sunny day In June 2005 I visited Jindo. We got on a bus
bound to Jindo at 7 a.m. It was quite a long journey of six

Jindo Bridge

hours, Under Kim Yeon-gap's guidance, we paid a visit to Kang Song-dae institution. Kim introduced to me. Kang who is a famous singer in Gwangju and Mokpo. Many drums and Janggu (a hourglass-shaped drum) showed the history.

After saying good bye to Kang, we met Park Byeong-hun who is a former director of Jindo Cultural Center. He has profound knowledge of Jindo Arirang and he was very instructive.

b. The Town of Jindo

Jindo is the third largest Island in South Korea, and is located Southwest of Korea. Jindo-gun consists of 225 islands.

It is facing Haenam to the east and many islands of Muan to the west. The south of Jindo is facing Jejudo Island. Mt. Cheomchalsan and Mt. Yeoguisan are located southeast of Jindo surrounding the city. These mountains decrease in elevation to the southwest allowing people to cultivate. The cultivated land takes up about 30% of the gross area of Jindo. The land is mostly hilly, and there run the two streams of Yoksil and Simgye making the area fertile enough to cultivate.

Originally, Jindo was called Injindo during the Baekje, but the name changed to Jindo after the Silla conquest. Jindo is a town of culture, so people say that "Never boast of your singing, writing and drawing in Jindo." This means the level of those arts is very high and this place has produced many artists of distinguished talent. Also, one of its precious natural products is the Jindo dog, designated as Natural Monument No. 53. This dog is the most famous of all Korean canines.

Historically, this is the place where Admiral Yi Sun-sin defeated the invading Japanese navy about 400 years ago during the Joseon Dynasty. As Jindo is adjacent to the ocean, it was invaded many times. Thus it is natural that people of Jindo are independent and strong. Additionally, the women of Jindo are very open-minded.

The characteristics of Jindo people influenced the formation of Jindo Arirang. The song of Jindo Arirang focuses on the farewell of the lover. Husbands and lovers often left to fight against the invaders, or went out to the seas for living. So the singer of Arirang should be female. Collectively, the mood of Jindo Arirang includes sorrow, longing, and even amusement.

c. Tales of Jindo Arirang

Jindo Arirang also has a tale. A man loved a lady living in the same village of Jindo. They had engaged to marry in the future. One day he needed to leave the town to make money for his living. He went to another town and started working on a farm owned by a rich family. The owner had a daughter. And the daughter fell in love with him. At that time, it was a dishonor for a lady from such a high class to date with a man from working class.

Her parents learned of the inappropriate relationship, and the couple had to leave the farm. They returned to his hometown, Jindo. Meanwhile, his original fiancée there was waiting for him to come back. She heard that he came back home with a lady who was from a rich family. She agonized with a broken heart, and sang a song to soothe her sorrow. The song became Jindo Arirang. The story consists of "Engagement→ Betrayal of man→Grief of woman." It is mainly about the lover's betrayal.

Jindo Arirang is mostly about love. Some of Jindo Arirang takes the form of conversation between a man and a woman. People say that when women singers sing Jindo Arirang, the song sounds more impressive. That's why Jindo Arirang is often called 'Women's song.' The feeling of a betrayed woman is the base of Jindo Arirang. The grudge of women from the tale eventually created a sorrowful song, Jindo Arirang.

d. Feature of Jindo Arirang

As to the musical features of Jindo Arirang, its scale is Jungmori jangdan. It has the characteristics of a feminine folksong: the narrator is a woman; it is a story of a woman. According to Professor Im Dong-gwon, "Jindo Arirang has enchanting music and powerful sound." The features of Jindo Arirang are :

① The name differs from other Arirang. Its full name is "Jindo Arirang taryeong" not "Jindo Arirang" based upon *Maecheonyarok* by Hwang Hyeon. Also, Arirang played in the Royal Court was called "Arirang taryeong."

② It has a broad range sound going up to a very high tone and then suddenly plunging to a very low tone. It also has a distinguished vibration: the sound breaks and explodes.

③ The words of the song are usually about the lover, but there are some parts about working or talking with a stranger on the street. Thus, Jindo Arirang is a song of living as well as of grudge and sorrow.

Jindo Arirang Monument

Finally, "Eung, Eung, and Eung~" in the refrain means 1) transformed snort, 2) sound of an amour, 3) sound of whining, 4) groaning from hard work, 5) the sound of grudge or resentment.

e. Sound of crying

There is a monument of Jindo Arirang in Mt. Cheomchalsan. "Jindo Arirang is foremost to sing by anybody and to listen to with pleasant thought. Jindo Arirang is the song which settles sadness and resentment with witty lyrics. Our ancestors of

Singing the song of Jindo Arirang(Kang Song-dae)

Jindo were wise to handle suffering of life by singing a song. We build this monument to show our proper pride in the tradition. We hope our descendants will remember the tradition and will be proud of it."

Consequently, the essence of Jindo Arirang is its poetic diction. There is the fine point of the tune which leads the lingering sound. And the degree of interest is higher than any other song of Arirang. Furthermore, the lyric of Jindo Arirang is diverse, and its tone is tasteful.

Singing the song of Jindo Arirang before the Park Jong-gi's Monument

f. Park Jong-gi and the Principal of Jindo Arirang

Jindo Arirang is also called 'Arirang taryeong." Let us assume from this name that Jindo Arirang was established during the Japanese occupation when the 'Taryeong' was very popular. For this reason, we neeed to pay attention to the role of Park Jong-gi(1879-1939).

According to some of Korean Intangible Cultural Properties (Park Jin-ju, Park Byeong-gu, Park Byeong-won, and Gu Chun-hong), Park Jong-gi wrote the lyrics and arranged the Jindo Arirang with the help of Park Ji-yeon, Park Dong-jun,

Chae Jung-in and Yang Dong-do in the early 1900s.

At that time Jindo Arirang was called by several different names such as Honam Arirang and Namdo Arirang. Park suggested that the song be called Jindo Arirang because mainly Jindo people sang the song. In addition, one episode made Jindo Arirang popular. Now I would like to talk about the historical story.

During the Japanese occupation, GGJ established "Joseon Shinto Shrine" to kill the spirit of Korea. At the opening ceremony of the Shrine(October 1925) noted singers and dancers were invited to celebrate the event. Park was among those. He played Jindo Arirang. Impressed by his performance, the chief of GGJ Saito Minoru danced to the song. Then he asked Park "Where is this song from?" Park answered "This is Jindo Arirang." At that time the song was broadcast everywhere through Gyeongseong Broadcasting System(the predecessor of KBS). Later the song was known to the world by prominent singers from Jindo. To conclude, Park played a great role in spreading Jindo Arirang to the rest of Korea and to the world.

5. The North Korean National Policy toward folksongs and Arirang

a. North Korea's Policy on folksongs

During Japanese rule of Korea, the Japanese employed a policy of obliterating the Korean local culture. Much of our nation's musical heritage was lost, and in its place, deeply-rooted remains of Japanese culture remained in everyday language and writing. Additionally, due to the long period of feudalistic customs and ideals, many folksongs and much of popular music, including Arirang, were considered to be inferior, and were disdained, even after liberation from Japan. It was at this time that North Korea took an active role to rediscover, preserve, and organize our people's musical heritage, starting with folksongs. On September 9, 1948, three years after liberation, North Korea began the policy of "The People's Democratic Revolution Against Imperialism and Feudalism," part of which was the "Definition of Music for the People." However, because of the confusion and the limited circumstances that ensued right after liberation, as well as the subsequent Korean War, the work of rediscovering and collecting folksongs, including the Arirang, was inevitably halted.

In the 1970s, North Korea began anew its policy for proceeding with the works. As a result of their investigations, *1,000 Joseon folksongs* was published in 2000 by the Pyongyang Consolidated Culture and Arts Press. This is a folksong book that contains the efforts made by North Korea after liberation to preserve the folksongs of our people.

North Korea' s policy regarding the rediscovery, preservation, and development of folksongs is the following :

We must inherit and develop the popular elements of the culture and arts of the past, and remove that which is unscientific and lowly. Some think that singing all the songs that were sung in the past is a folksong heritage, but this is certainly mistaken. This tendency is at odds with our basic route for developing our people's folksong culture. In the fields of folksongs, music, dance, and many others, we must first preserve the unique and superior characteristic that we have, and at the same time, create a new rhythm, melody, and movement that modern life requires. We must learn how to incorporate new content into the abundant and diverse cultural forms our people possess.

In this sense, the North Korean government defined folksongs as a musical heritage, created through the wisdom of the masses people as they lived a long period of laboral and social life. It also defined subclassifications of folksongs, such as songs sung while working, called work songs, and songs praising patriotism and the beauty of the motherland, called lyrical folksongs.

b. North Korean folksongs and Arirang

Folksongs have been produced in each region, and this is true in North Korea as well. There are a variety of folksongs developed in each region. I will list the folksongs that are well known in North Korea currently. First, Seodo Arirang, which is well known in the western regions, in Pyeongan-do and Hwanghae-do Province.

In Pyeongan-do Province we find the Yonggang Ginari, Yeongbyeonga, and Baebaengigut. In the Hwanghae-do Province area, there's the Yangsando, Doraji, Jangsangot taryeong, and Haeju Arirang, in the Haeju area. In the Hamgyeong-do Province area, there's Dondollari in the Bukcheong region, and in the Namcheong area, Dancheon Arirang, and in Hamgyeongbuk-do Province, Onseong Arirang and Musan Arirang.

In Jagang-do Province, Arirang is popular, and in Gangwon-do Province, Gangwon-do Arirang, Tongcheon Arirang, Goseong Arirang, Samilpo Arirang, and Singosan taryeong (Wonsan Arirang). Among these, songs such as Yangsando, Doraji, Yeongbyeonga, and Baegyeonpokpo were inherited and developed to this day as chorus songs, dance songs, orchestral music, and a variety of other formats.

After liberation, the most popular among the Arirang of the time was Bonjo Arirang, sung by singer Wang Su-bok. Then in 1958, for the 10th Anniversary of the Republic, singer Kang Ung-kyong of "My Glorious Country", a musical performance with 3,000 participants, sang Gin Arirang, which was later sung by many other folk singers. Yonggang Ginari was used as the basis for a new song, Harvest Year Has Come to Cheongsanri Beol, which was rated as a national hit. This song was also performed as an orchestra song in the 1970s.

On the other hand, the representative song of Pyeongan-do area, Susimga, was said to "reflect the emptiness of the city dweller's everyday life by lamenting the lonely passions of the separating men and women", and was deemed unfitting of the proper daily emotion of the people. Aewonseong of Hamgyeong-do Province area was also evaluated as being improper for singing of extreme sadness, or han, and was not properly passed down.

In the 1970s, North Korea's musical world experienced an age of Revolutionary Songs. These Revolutionary Songs had a revolutionary contents, and were created in the style of North Korea. They are sometimes named after their representative song, Pibada-or Blood Bath-Revolutionary Songs. The original work of Pibada was a play performed during the 1930s, during the struggle against Japanese rule. In early 1970s, North Korea had five Revolutionary Songs, including Pibada,

Flowering Virgin, True Daughter of the Party, Talk to Me, Jungle, and The Song of Mt. Geumgangsan. The North Korean government advertised these songs widely, and they were played both domestically and internationally.

Later, the Hwansanggok (composed by Choi Song-han), or "Fantasy Song", based on Bonjo Arirang, was performed, piquing interest in Arirang once again. This song later became the orchestral piece representative of North Korea. This song was also played in Seoul in 2001, with a joint performance by the North Korean National Orchestra and the KBS Orchestra. When the New York Philharmonic Orchestra, directed by Lorin Maazel, first performed at Pyongyang and Seoul, this Arirang was also performed.

So far, we have looked at the folksongs and Arirang of North Korea. There is much more to say about the North Korean Arirang singers as well. However, the intent of this book is to not divide the South and North, and to explain how the 70 million united people sing the Arirang. The tale of the Arirang singers will have to wait until next time. More importantly, we must focus on the fact that whether in South Korea or in North Korea, or even outside the Korean Peninsula, all Korean people sing the Arirang folksong out loud, and live lives that elevate the status of our people. Therefore, I would like to describe the most popular Arirang in North Korea in the following manner.

6. Haeju Arirang

Korean

아리 아리 얼싸 아라리요

아리랑 얼씨구 넘어가세

아리랑 고개는 웬 고갠가

넘어갈 듯 넘어올 듯 근심이로다

Romanization

A ri A ri eol ssa A ra ri yo

A ri rang eol ssi gu neom eo ga se

A ri rang go gae neun wen go gaen ga

Neom eo gal deut neom eo ol deut geun sim i ro da

English

Ari Ari eolssa Arariyo

Arirang eolssigu let us walk through

What is this, the Arirang pass?

It's a worry, coming and going alike

Haeju Arirang

Delightfully(Yangsando Rhythm)

mf

A ri a ri - eol- ssa- A- ra ri - yo

A ri rang- eol- ssi gu- neom eo- ga- se-

A ri rang- go- gae neun- wen- go gaen- ga
What is this, the Arirang pass?

Neom eo gal deut- neom eo ol deut- geun sim i ro da
It's a worry, coming and going alike

Korean

수양산 진달래 만발한데
님하고 나하고 꽃구경 가세

뒷동산 개나리 파두세 좋고
정든 님 얼굴은 보두세 좋네

바람아 광풍아 불지를 마라
추풍에 낙엽이 다 떨어진다

The Legend of Haeju Arirang

Haeju Arirang is the representative song in Hwanghae-do Province. This song of Arirang is a reflection of love between man and woman. Therefore, the melody is bright and cheerful.

The characteristic feature of Haeju Arirang is its very harmoniously arranged set of melody and refrain which allows to manage the vocal variation. In this song, the refrain is positioned at the beginning part to emphasize its own high tune. This type of structure is only we can see in Haeju Arirang. That is to say, this is the very specific feature of Arirang of Seodo Region, North Korea.

The melody of Haeju Arirang is similar with that Musan Arirang in Hamgyeong-do Province and Miryang Arirang. Haeju Arirang and Miryang Arirang have a very similar rhythm too. But its structure is very unique iteself.

7. Seodo Arirang

Korean

아리랑 아리랑 아라리요
아리랑 고개를 넘어간다
간다 간다 나는 간다
님을 따라서 나는 간다

Romanization

A ri rang A ri rang A ra ri yo
A ri rang go gae reul neom eo gan da
Gan da gan da nan eun gan da
Nim eul tta ra seo na neun gan da

English

Arirang Arirang Arariyo
Walking through Arirang Pass
Walking through, walking through
Walking through following my love

Seodo Arirang

Arirang- Arirang- A ra ri- yo

A ri rang- go gae- reul- neom- eo- gan da-
Walking through Arirang Pass

Gan da gan- da- na neun- gan da-
Walking through,   walking through

Nim eul- tta ra- seo- na- neun- gan- da-
Walking through following my love

Korean

저기야 향산에 비 맞은 제비

수풀 속에 떠네

저기야 향산에 박달나무

홍두깨 방망이로 다 나간다

홍두깨 방망이로 다 나가면

큰애기 손질에 다 녹는다

팔랑 팔랑 수갑사 댕기는
어깨야 넘어서 춤을 춘다

노다가소 노다가소
저 달이 지도록 노다가소

청사초롱 불 밝혀라
그립던 낭군이 들어온다

The feature of Seodo Arirang

Seodo Arirang as a Korean folksong depicting a romantic relationship between a man and a woman was originated from Hwanghae-do Province area and has been widely disseminated to Korea's Seodo and Central regions.

This folksong is one of the oldest one among other song of Arirang because it came from a legend of Seongbu and Yi Rang which was based on historical facts in the early years of the Joseon Dynasty.

Seodo Arirang was refined and completed in the process of being favorably sung by ordinary Korean people a long time.

8. Dancheon Arirang

Korean

아라리요 아라리요

아리랑 띄여루

배 몰아주세 아리아리랑 스리스리랑

아라리요 아리랑

띄여루 배 몰아주세

Romanization

A ra ri yo A ra ri yo

A ri rang ttui yeo ru

Bae mo ra ju se A ri a ri rang seu ri seu ri rang

A ra ri yo A ri rang

ttui yeo ru bae mo ra ju se

English

Arariyo Arariyo

Arirang, flowing, rowing the boat

Ari Ari Arirang Seuri Seuri Seurirang Arariyo

Arirang, flowing, rowing the boat

Dancheon Arirang

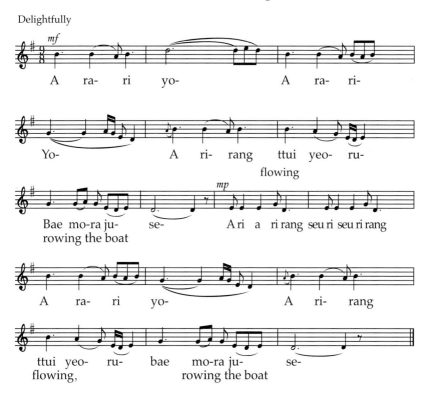

Delightfully

A ra- ri yo- A ra- ri-

Yo- A ri- rang ttui yeo- ru-
flowing

Bae mo-ra ju- se- A ri a ri rang seu ri seu ri rang
rowing the boat

A ra- ri yo- A ri- rang

ttui yeo- ru- bae mo-ra ju- se-
flowing, rowing the boat

Korean

갈매기야 너도 좋아 춤을 추느냐

아리랑 띄여루 만선이로세

The formation of Dancheon Arirang

Dancheon Arirang came from Dancheon region and became popular in many areas of Hamgyeong-do Provinces. It describes a love relationship between a single man and a single woman in fishing environment.

In Dancheon Arirang there was a legend of Gopgye and Yi Rang relating to its origin. Once upon a time, at a fishing village in Dancheon there were a single man named Yi Rang and a single woman named Gopgye, making their livelihood by fishing using a rented boat owned by Hwang Ji-seon. Even though Yi Rang had been engaged in exacting labor like fishing with his father in the rough sea and led a life in poverty, he took care of housekeeping of Gopgye who was left fatherless and barely made a living with her mother. In these circumstances, they gradually fell in love each other.

Because Mr. Hwang, the boat owner, coveted a more beautifully matured Gopgye, he attempted to stop the couple from loving. Because of Mr. Hwang's insidious wiles, Gopgye could not help but go through the twists and turns of her life that deeply hurt her feelings and Yi Rang too had several time near-death experience. At long last Yi Rang could settle the matter and make a happy family.

The melody of Dancheon Arirang is closer to the Seodo Arirang in the beginning part of the song and is similar to Arirang sung in Namdo regions in the main part of the sung. This tells us that Dancheon Arirang was created under the influence by in Seodo as well as Namdo regions.

9. Goseong Arirang

Korean

서산에 지는 해는 지고 싶어서 지나

나를 버리고 가는 님은 가고 싶어서 가나

아리아리랑 스리스리랑 아라리요

아리랑 고개로 나를 넘겨주소

Romanization

Seo san e ji neun hae neun ji go sip eo seo ji na

Na reul beo ri go ga neun nim eun ga go sip eo seo ga na

A ri a ri rang seu ri seu ri rang a ra ri yo

A ri rang go gae ro na reul neom gyeo ju so

English

The sun that sets to the west, does it set willingly?

Does my love, leaving me, do so willingly?

Ari Arirang Seuri Seurirang Arariyo

Let me walk through Arirang Pass

Goseong Arirang

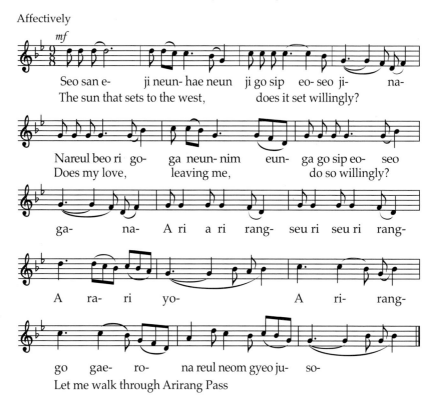

Affectively

Seo san e- ji neun- hae neun ji go sip eo- seo ji- na-
The sun that sets to the west, does it set willingly?

Nareul beo ri go- ga neun- nim eun- ga go sip eo- seo
Does my love, leaving me, do so willingly?

ga- na- A ri a ri rang- seu ri seu ri rang-

A ra- ri yo- A ri- rang-

go gae- ro- na reul neom gyeo ju- so-
Let me walk through Arirang Pass

Korean

먼동이 튼다네 먼동이 튼다네

님 그려 꾸던 꿈은 다 깨어져 버렸네

The Tales of Goseong Arirang

These lyrics were included in the 1931 publication of the Chosun Popular Songs (Editor: Chosun Lyrics Institute). The verses "Fight and fight, and when I can fight no more / I will set the whole world afire" was struck out with black ink. Songs like these spread through the country through popular singers.

As the Japanese occupation became more serious, the farmers who had lost their lands immigrated to Manchuria or Primorskiy in Russia. Through them, the stories of the struggle for independence against Japan in far away lands, such as the plains of Manchuria and the mountain ranges around Mt. Baekdusan spread to Korea, and their influence can be seen in Korean folksongs, such as the Arirang above. However, lyrics with too-strong anti-Japanese sentiments were deleted during the revisions.

10. After Watching
the Arirang Mass Games

I had known of the Arirang Mass Games through newspapers, magazines, and television, and had imagined it many times in my heart. Finally, on October 5, 2011, I was able to witness it live in May Day Stadium, on Neungnado Islet in the Daedonggang River, in Pyongyang, in the company of over 100,000 other viewers. This is a brief summary of my experience.

The Arirang Mass Games trace the sorrows, joys, laughs, and happiness in the history of a nation. It struck me that this could be a great opportunity for foreigners, with their limited knowledge of Korea, to perhaps catch a glimpse of who we truly are.

When we think of North Korea, we can't suppress the surge of thoughts of a political character. However, the content itself of the Arirang Mass Games stays apart from any political ideology, and focuses instead on creating the ultimate artistic expression. That's how it draws the viewer into the ecstasy of the moment. At the same time, it was also worth noting that the North Korean hosts were doing everything possible to ensure that every convenience was provided to the viewers of the Mass Games.

This show of sensitivity and convenience was a display of the beautiful decorum and courtesy of our people. In short, the proceeding of the Games was a clean and orderly display of immaculate cooperation.

North Korea often uses the Mass Games as a celebration of Kim Il-sung, their supreme leader, and as a friendly art festival. But at the same time, it seemed to be a message of peace to the international community. It was being showcased as a beautiful artistic event, showing a longing for peace, away from foreign invasion.

I have heard that the Arirang Mass Games are criticized as being political in nature. Some hold the view that a festival of such a scale as this one can only be for the purpose of gaining foreign currency or for strengthening the existing political system. I believe that the validity of those statements depends on each individual's point of view. But in any case, it is a fact that North Korea is making a great effort through this event in the social endeavor of tourism, and that the amount of manpower required for an event of this scale can only be mustered due to the unique situation in North Korea. However, when we compare and contrast the positives and the negatives, it is clearly undeniable that Arirang is truly outstanding from a purely artistic point of view.

Above all, as an Arirang scholar, the question I want to ask

A performance of the Arirang Mass Games in May Day Stadium sites on Neungnado Island in the Daedonggang River.

is this-Why the Arirang? If the purpose was merely to advertise and to mobilize, to provide a spectacle, there must have been other topics of a much grander scale. Why did North Korea necessarily choose the Arirang as the main title for their festival?

A few years ago, my endeavors to gain further insight on the Arirang Festival led me to the South American country of Brazil-more specifically, the world-famous Carnival in Rio. I could tell right away that Brazil had made great efforts to accommodate the visitors pouring in from all over the world. The Brazilian efforts to run the Carnival every single year, striving to improve its quality, and the painstaking care taken by the government in particular cannot be defiled by the declaration that it is only for the purpose of gaining money. I could see that their efforts stemmed from their desire to make their artistry in the Samba known to all their international guests.

Albeit in a different way, the Arirang Mass Games also show an unrivaled content in artistic and cultural expression. The mass gymnastics and the artistic performance of the Arirang Mass Games are undeniably world-class material. In particular, witnessing the spectators entering the stadium without the slightest trace of disorder is, by itself, clear proof that the Arirang Mass Games is something more than just a source of income, but the formation of a cultural phenomenon that guarantees high artistry and the opens a new chapter in world culture.

What other festivals are there to make Arirang known to the world? My heart is filled with the longing that, through the peaceful reconciliation and reunification of the two Koreas, that the 70 million Koreans may join in an Arirang festival of peace recognized by the world.

The Diffusion of Arirang

Samjiyeon Pond located in the near the Mt. Baekdusan

7

Chapter

1. Domestic

a. Restoration of Gyeongbokgung Palace

The important role of the reconstruction of the Gyeongbok-gung Palace under the regentship of the Daewongun as a crucible in the formation and diffusion of Arirang has already been discussed. Now other factors in spreading this national folksong will be studied.

b. Transfer by Raftsmen

Timbers were delivered on Bukhangang or Namhangang River. To build government offices, and the governor's residence, high quality woods were needed. The materials from Jeongseon were best of the best because Jeongseon was surrounded by deep forest. Moreover, there was a river that made the transportation to Seoul easier. The rafts of Bukhangang River departed from the Hapgang River in Inje, Gangwon-do Province, and stopped over in Chuncheon to supply workers.

As men gathered in knots, there were women whose job

was to entertain the men. Jajin Arari was sung by the women entertainers and the workers(raftsmen). The song of Jajin Arari drifted over the country following the rafters and the ladies. The raft of Namhangang River departed from Auraji, Jeongseon where the streams of Songcheon and Goljicheon merge. During the transportation, a long Arari was sung. This song was sung by the ladies and workers to make the work more fun.

c. Diffusion by Singers

In addition, many noted singers sang the song of Jeongseon Arirang while traveling all over the places. Naturally, the song of Jeongseon Arirang was spread to every corner of the country. The celebrated singers of Inje, Gangwon-do were Ko Deok-myeong, Kim Cheon-yu and Park Sun-tae. They traveled in Wonsan and Hoeryeong singing the song.

d. Distribution of Folksong

I like to summarize the distribution of folksong of Korea as follows :

① Any area dwelled by the Yangban class(the aristocratic class) only: there was no folksong reported. Virtually the aristocratic class used to ignore the song of Arirang.
② In the interior region and the coastal areas: there were folksong handed down to the people. But Arirang thrived in the farming areas of the interior rather than in

the coast areas.

③ In the farm village: the labor class(working class) loved the folksong more than the leisured class did. This phenomenon indicates the relationship between the class and their cultural taste.

④ In the poor farm village: few folksongs were transmitted from generation to generation.

⑤ Generally speaking, the fertile farm land and the center of the administrative district usually kept a large number of folksong.

e. Prohibition on Singing Arirang under Japanese Occupation

The film *Arirang* produced by Na Un-gyu premiered on the screen at Dansungsa Theater in October 1, 1926 when the building of the GGJ was completed. The film *Arirang* comprised the grudge of the Korean people, who were taken from their land by Japanese Totaku Joint Stock Company and the hardship of the Korean migrants who were expelled to foreign countries such as Manchuria.

Thus, the song of Arirang was prohibited from being sung at that time. Today this song of Arirang is sung by people over the world. As mentioned above, people were prohibited all singing Arirang by the GGJ in 1929. The GGJ tightened the censorship over the songs and the thoughts in 1933, and finally banned teaching Korean in 1938. On the other hand, the

GGJ composed martial songs and distributed them to educational institutions in 1939. The GGJ exercised control over publications, especially, on Korean songs and Korean ideologies. The Bureau of GGJ considered the Korean folksong like Arirang as anti-Japanese propaganda.

Koreans were prohibited from singing not only the song of Arirang but also the National Anthem publically for security reasons. The *Sangnoksu* (meaning evergreen) was also banned because of its rebellious words. And '*Goodbye, Joseon*' (Columbia) recorded by Richard Choi who was born in Hawaii and performed several times in New York was also banned for security reasons. The records were confiscated and sealed up.

As mentioned above, people could not sing the song of Arirang. However, who could stop Koreans from singing the song of Korea, the song of their hearts. Today Arirang of Korea survived and rose again. Arirang is now considered as the song of the nation and of the world. The more severe the oppression got, the stronger Koreans grew.

When visiting Seoul, Korea on Octover 31, 2008 to collect the data on Arirang, I had a chance to see the performance played by the National Pops Orchestra-Yeomin (Conductor Kim Man-seok) at the National Gugak Center in Seoul, Korea. Nine songs were selected from the songs prohibited during the Japanese occupation, including Arirang and the National Anthem.

2. International Diffusion

According to the Korean Ministry of Foreign Affairs And Trade, seven hundred million overseas Koreans reside in 170 countries in the world (2009). Even if their lives may differ by location, they have one thing in common: they sing the song of Arirang. Thus I think that they are the messengers who transfer the song of Arirang to the world. I would like to explain about the diffusion of the song of Arirang to Japan, China, Russia, America and Europe.

a. Japan

There are 900,000 Korean residents in Japan. Even though World War II was over nearly 65 years ago, the Koreans in Japan have not been emancipated in a sense. They still use the Japanese names instead of Korean names because they need to hide their origin so as not to be treated unfairly in Japan. Korean Japanese are discriminated against while they go to school. Even after they graduate from school, they have hardships getting a job. The 'Hitachi case' in 1970 is a good example of the discrimination. Park Jong-seok, a Korean living in Japan passed the employment exam of Hitachi Corporation, but later the company turned down his employment because he was a Korean.

To Japan, the song of Arirang is a very complicated issue. It is like the political difficulty between Korea and Japan. The song of Arirang was conveyed to Japan by the eight routes as follows :

① Articles and writings by Shinobu Junpei, the director of Incheon Port Authority. He wrote about Korea after he visited Korea around 1883.

② A radio program on Arirang produced by Joseon Broadcasting Corporation(JODK) and broadcasted by NHK(Japan Broadcasting Corporation) in 1936.

③ A record *Arirang No Wuda*(the song of Arirang) arranged by Koga Masao and sung by Iwaya Noriko and Hasekawa Ichiro

④ Korean students and workers in Japan

⑤ Tsushima Festival

⑥ Itsuki's Lullaby and Arirang

⑦ Kusano Taeko's book

⑧ Miyatsuka Toshiyo's book

Based upon this, I elaborated on Arirang in Japan as follow :

aa. Overseas Workers and Students

As mentioned already, compulsory Korean workers diffused the song of Arirang in Japan while comforting themselves. Additionally, some Koreans went to Japan to study or to find a new job. The song of Arirang was diffused by them as well. Other Korean folksongs were introduced to Japan along with the song of Arirang. But the song of Arirang became the song of Korea and gained popularity in Japan. You can find the song of Arirang in postcards or daily utensils of the time. Moreover, scribbles in Korean like "I missed you, Mom." or "When can I pass the Arirang Pass?" have been found on the walls of an old factory. The song of Arirang was not a mere song for many Korean workers under the Japanese occupation. It was one of their means to comfort their hard life.

bb.Tsushima Arirang Festival

Tsushima is located between Korea and Kyushu, Japan. It is 49.5 km from Busan, Korea. This Island belongs to Nagasaki Prefecture and consists of two Islands, Kamishima and Shimoshima. During the first weekend in August every year, Arirang Festival is held to pay a tribute to the first arrival of Joseon's envoys in Tsushima 400 years ago. Due to it's geographical location, Tsushima acted as a go-between Korea and Japan. Because the land of Tsushima was not fertile, Tsushima served the kings of Korea and received rice and beans in return since the Goryeo Dynasty.

Tsushima Arirang Festival

From 17th century to 19th century, the Joseon Dynasty sent envoys 12 times to the Shogunate of Japan to promote good neighborly relations. They landed in Tsushima first. This exchange of visits (Japan sent its envoys 5 times) enriched the culture of Japan. In the period of the 17th century to 19th century. Busan was an assembly place for various culture. It was also a symbol of friendship between Korea and Japan. However, today Busan does not retain a vestige of the cultural exchange. On the other hand, there are many traces left in Tsushima, and Arirang Festival has kept the memory of the historical event.

During this festival, the entire island goes back to the 19th century. At noon, *Mugunghwa*(the Rose of Sharon, national flower of Korea) and *Spring of Hometown*, two popular Korean songs ring all over the town. Tsushima respects Korea so that there is a neighborly amity between them. Before the cultural exchange, it is said that Tsushima had neither its own language nor customs. Thanks to the envoys from Korea, Tsushima learned painting, the Korean language, and so on.

People from various backgrounds participate in the festival. Professional dancers, musicians and students who are interested in the event take part. I think that this festival contributes to building the cultural diplomacy between two countries. However, some Japanese insist that Japanese culture surpasses that of Korea and they do not want the cultural exchange with Korea. I hope that this festival will help them understand the history. Moreover, I believe that the spirit of good neighborbood in the song of Arirang will accelerate the cultural exchange between Korea and Japan.

cc. Koga Masao's Music and Korea

In 1904, Koga Masao was born in Okawa, Fukuoka

Prefecture. When he was 7 years old, he moved to Incheon, Korea with his single mother. He went to an ordinary elementary school in Incheon. Through out his childhood, he was in constant contact with Korean music. When he was 12 years old, he moved with his mother to Seoul and entered Sunrin High School. During his high school days, he became distinguished in music playing in a school band. After graduation, he returned to Japan with his mother.

As he spent quite a long time in Korea, he had many chances to be acquainted with Korean culture. He said, "If I hadn't spent my boyhood in Korea, it wouldn't have been possible to create songs like *The flower is a flower*" right before he died in 1977. He confessed that his music was based on his experience in Korea. As mentioned already, his music was very closely bound up with Korea. His boyhood was far from happy. Poverty made him babysit after school. But his weary life in Korea became his musical property. It helped produce lots of sorrowful songs is "Sun Drops."

Evening primrose and "Sake wa Namidaka Tame Iki Ka? (Is sake a tear or a sigh?)" were created in loneliness and hardships in Korea. Korean people as well as Japanese loved to sing his songs. I think that is because the Japanese and Korean have something in common. Koga Masao played an important role in spreading the song of Arirang to Japan. He arranged the original Arirang he heard in his boyhood for his style of Arirang. And then his Arirang was a great hit in Japan.

Koga Masao

On the other hand, Sato Sonosuke, the writer of the Japanese verson of Arirang did not have any relationship with the original Arirang of Korea.

However, from May 13, 1928 to June 20, 1928 he traveled around Manchuria. At that time, he visited Seoul, Gyeongju and Pyongyang. I assume that he might have been affected by Korean culture when he wrote the songs.

Koga loved Korea very much and fully understand the emotion of Korean people. I like to briefly summarize his article in *kaizo* (December 1932) as follows:

"Korea is my second hometown and I grew up over there. So it was possible for me to study music and compose songs. I was fascinated with the beautiful melody of the song of Arirang. Without discontinuing and ending lingering sound and sentimental mood is imbued into the chest, and it turns into a sad tone. This kind of mood of the song of Arirang is the one of unique features in Korea. Sometimes Korean people assumed that the song of Arirang is connected with the Arirang Pass, but it was originated in the tale of Arang, a daughter of the Magiatrate of Miryang."

Although Koga Masao's boyhood was hard, his music seems to have Joseon's sentiment, because his music career started while he was staying in Joseon. When he lived in Incheon, Joseon, he received an instrument 'Daejeonggeum' (a Korean string instrument) as a present from his cousin. That was his first encounter with music. Additionally, during his high school days, he received another present, a mandolin from Hisachiro, who was his other cousin. Then, he was fascinated by music. The encounter with the mandolin enabled him to organize a band in Meiji University and motivated him to become a composer. His mandolin and relics are still in the Koga Masao Memorial House in Tokyo, Japan.

In 1950, Koga Masao wrote a song '*Janggu of Tear.*' A theme of this song was a tragic nation which was divided into two countries after World War II, and the mood of the song was based on Arirang. Successively, in April 1950, Columbia, a record company, released a new record *Arirang and Doraji*. It is worth remembering that lots of Korean songs were produced by Japanese before and after the Korean War. According to Mitsuha Gazuo, Korean songs which were produced during the Korean War attracted Japanese. Among the songs, Itsuki's Lullaby was most popular, so it was called *The song of the Wandering Korean* or *Arirang of Japan*.

These days, there are a lot of pupils of Koga Masao in Japan. Singers Ookawa and Gobayashi succeeded to him and held a 'centennial anniversary for Koga Masao.'

The Encyclopedia of Japanese Music noted that Koga Masao composed Arirang. So it was asked for correction. He did not compose the song of Arirang but arranged Arirang in tune of Japanese. However, this fact shows his strong relationship with the song of Arirang. Because he had understood the meaning of the song of Arirang while he spent his boyhood in Korea, he could arrange and recreate the song of Arirang in Japan, and the song touched the Japanese hearts.

Let us list the most famous versions of Arirang as follows: the Japanese and English versions

アリランの唄

1. アリラン アリラン アラリヨ　　　　共
   アリラン峠を越えゆく　　　　　　　共
   涙こぼれて 花咲け　　　　　　　　淡
   君と分かれて 行く空　　　　　　　淡
   アリラン アリラン アラリヨ　　　　共
   アリラン峠を越えゆく　　　　　　　共

2. アリラン アリラン アラリヨ　　　　略
   アリラン峠を越えゆく　　　　　　　略
   胸のなやみ つきせず　　　　　　　長
   星のかずは 知れずに　　　　　　　長
   アリラン アリラン アラリヨ　　　　共
   アリラン峠を越えゆく　　　　　　　共

3. アリラン アリラン アラリヨ　　　略

　アリラン峠を越えゆく　　　　　略

　草も泣くよ 夜風に　　　　　　淡

　われも 泣くよ 夜露　　　　　　淡

　アリラン アリラン アラリヨ　　　共

　アリラン峠を越えゆく　　　　　共

4. アリラン アリラン アラリヨ　　　略

　アリラン峠を越えゆく　　　　　略

　明日は ひとり いづこに　　　　長

　戀しの君 夢に見よ　　　　　　長

　アリラン アリラン アラリヨ　　　共

　アリラン峠を越えゆく　　　　　共

Song of Arirang Pass*

Arirang Arirang Arariyo (Duet)

Over Arirang Pass I go. (Duet)

Tears, into flowers bloom (Solo)

Parting with you under dark skies (Solo)

Arirang Arirang Arariyo (Duet)

Over Arirang Pass I go. (Duet)

Arirang Arirang Arariyo (Tacet)

Over Arirang Pass I go. (Tacet)

Without end does my heart ache (Solo)

Without limit does star dust spread (Solo)

Arirang Arirang Arariyo (Duet)

Over Arirang Pass I go. (Duet)

Arirang Arirang Arariyo (Tacet)

Over Arirang Pass I go.(Tacet)

In the night's wind grasses cry, (Solo)

Shedding dew drops, I too cry. (Solo)

Arirang Arirang Arariyo (Duet)

Over Arirang Pass I go. (Duet)

Arirang Arirang Arariyo (Solo)

Over Arirang Pass I go. (Solo)

Tomorrow, all alone, where will I (Solo)

See you, love, in my dream? (Solo)

Arirang Arirang Arariyo (Duet)

Over Arirang Pass I go. (Duet)

*touched up by Professor Kachi Yukio

I recently read an interesting writing by a Japanese music critic. The general Nabeshima Naoshige, who participated in the Japanese Invasion of Korea (1592-1598) under orders of Toyotomi Hideyoshi, took Hong Ho-yeon, who was the son of a Confucian scholar, as a slave, and took him to Saga. As Hong grew up, he was recognized for his intelligence, and found work in Saga. However, at the age of 70, he missed his motherland, and asked for permission to return to Joseon. Nabeshima Katsushige, the daimyo at the time, allowed his return. However, as Hong Ho-yeon awaited the ship to Joseon at the port, the daimyo sent someone to escort him back. Hong Ho-yeon lived in Japan for the rest of his life. Hong Ho-yeon's descendants have branched out into various family names. Among them is the first name 'Koga', and Koga Masao, a renown musician in Japanese popular music, is also Hong Ho-yeon's descendant.

dd. Kim Yeong-gil's Song of Arirang on the Boat headed for North Korea

On a severe snowstorm day, a famous singer from Japan was leaving the port of Niigata, Japan for North Korea. And he started singing the song of Arirang on ship. Nagata Kenjiro sang the song of Arirang at the turning point of his life identifying himself as Korean. He was Kim Yeong-gil. I found information about Kim in the book of *Arirang Journey of 8 Provinces* by Kim Yeon-gap, and cited by Miyatsuka Toshio, Arirang researcher. Kim Yeong-gil appeared to have an unfortunate professional life. I would like to briefly trace his path based upon the two researchers.

First, let us look at the newspaper of Mainichi Shinbun of January 30, 1960:

The 6th returning fleet having 998 people aboard left from the port of Niigata to North Korea on January 29. Due to a snowstorm warning, the ships departed three hours behind the schedule. Also a tenor Nagata Kenjiro (49) of Fujiwara Opera Company got on the ship with about 350 Korean students of Yokohama seeing him off. He made a dramatic scene by singing the song of Arirang before the ship set off.

At that time, sending Koreans to North Korea was a controversial issue. So it was an unprecedented incident that a Korean who was returning to North Korea sang the song of Arirang on the ship. He was born in North Korea in 1909. He moved to Japan in 1928, and went to military school where he majored in the clarinet. After he graduated as top on the list, he took part in many music contests. When he used a Japanese name, Nagata Kenjiro, he got a prize. However, one day, when using his Korean name he received a prize of second place. It meant he could not win the first place, If he was Korean. So the sponsor instantly decided to give him a second place prize.

Fortunately, he received much recognition from the most famous singer of Japan, Miura Tamaki. This incident changed his life as a professional singer. The famous singer Miura picked him up as her partner for the opera *Madam Butterfly*, for which he won great fame in Japan.

In 1945, Korea was liberated from the Japanese occupation. Many Koreans in Japan needed to decide whether to leave or stay. Kim Yeong-gil was one of them, and he decided to go back to his country leaving his fame in Japan. In January 1960, he made up his mind to move to North Korea with all his family, and he held a farewell concert just ten days before leaving. Some Korean songs were included in the concert program. The second and the third parts of the concert were Arirang, Motherland, and Korean tunes.

I would like to point out that he sang the song of Arirang at the turning point of his life. Although he became a famous singer in Japan by hiding his nationality, he wanted to find himself and to identify himself as Korean. At the turning point, he sang the song of Arirang, revealing himself as Korean. Under the Japanese occupation, many Korean artists including Choe Seung-hui, who was one of the greatest dancers of that time played a conspicuous part in spreading the song of Arirang to Japan.

ee. Arirang library of Hayashi Eidai

Before the end of World War II, Japan enlisted young Korean men and women to bring to the war place. The young men worked at mines and at the construction sites of military facilities and roads. The young women were victimized as sex slaves for the Japanese soldiers in the war. Hayashi Eidai, a Japanese writer was looking to trace the Korean victims in World War II. The war had ended 60 years previously. Why did he want to research and write about it? Even the Japanese government took notice of his works. He finally published a book *Arirang Pass, not appearing on*

The book cover of Hayashi Eidai

the Map.

I read this book in 2006 and appreciated his effort very much. Without his work, the stories of Korean victims could be forgotton forever. I also read about his father's story. It was so sad. His father was tortured to death because he hid runaway Korean miners in his house. When Hayashi was young, he lived near Tsukuho Mine in Kitakyushu. His father, Doraji was a chief priest of a shrine in an old village. He sometimes accompanied his father to the Shinto Shrine to pray. One day, when he put on his shoes to go into the shrine, he found that there were several miners hiding in a small space under the floor. They were frightened to see him. Hayashi asked his father about the strangers under the floor.

"Dad, who are they under the floor?"

His father did not answer right away. After a while, his father talked to him.

"They are Koreans who were forced to work in the mine. Many of them die in the mine because the mine is not a safe place to work and they're originally farmers not miners. They ran away for their lives."

His father sympathized with them. Thereafter, there were always 4-5 runaway miners hiding in his house. Hayashi's father provided them with food and shelter until they found another place to hide. Hayashi Doraji had had a good reason to help runaway Koreans. When he was young, he was called into the dispatch troops in Siberia(1918-1922). The intense cold of Siberia was the most unendurable suffering. Many Japanese suffered from frostbite. At that time, Koreans who lived in Siberia helped them heal their frozen hands and feet. Doraji had heard the story from one of his fellows. He could not forget the kindness of Koreans. Thus he hid the Korean miners in his house, and helped them escape safely.

However, the Japanese police were not happy with his behavior. They arrested him on a charge of covering the escapees. He was tortured to death in a jail. After the war, the US Army entered Japan. One day, two Koreans visited Eidai's house. They came to meet his father, Doraji, who helped them get away from the miserable mine. They mourned over the death of his father. They shed tears and left 2 dollars in Hayashi's hand. Hayashi attached the two dollars to the wall to remember the lessons of his dad's benevolence. The two dollars motivated him to work for the suffered Koreans and his late father's society during the war time in Japan. He is still doing his research on *Compulsory Korean labor*, and he is in charge of the "Arirang Library" which has considerable data of Arirang.

ff. The Suicide squad Tak Gyeong-hyeon

There is the song of Arirang with grief in Japan. Arirang is a curious song. Some times they sing Arirang in the jaws of death. There is something special in the song. During World War II, as a member of the suicide squad of Japan, a Korean pilot Tak Gyeong-hyeon ended his youthful life in the sky of Okinawa. Before he went to die he sang the song of Arirang.

He was born in Sacheon, Gyeongsangnam-do Province, Korea on November 15, 1920. When he was young, his family moved to Kyoto, Japan. In 1938, he changed his name into a Japanese name, Mitsuyama. In October 1943, he entered the Chiran Aviation School as a pilot trainee after he graduated from Kyoto Pharmaceutical College. Chiran was a base of the suicide squad. In 1945, there was a severe fight in Okinawa to protect the main land of Japan.

Chiran was the closest airfield to Okinawa, so it was in the spearhead of the war. The squad of 431 pilots launched mass attacks against the invading troops. About 20 percent of 2500 soldiers died in the war of Okinawa. Eleven of them were young Koreans.

We know the real names of only four Koreans; Takayama Noboru, first lieutenant(23), Mitsuyama Fumitaka (Tak Gyeong-hyeon), second lieutenant(24), Mutsugi, Hisashi second lieutenant(24), Ookawa Masahaki(18).

Now history has not left any record for the rest of them. However, I found records about Tak Gyeong-hyeon. He used to visit a restaurant of Tomiya in front of the school. And he kept a good relationship with Torihama Tome who was the owner of the restaurant and her daughter, Reiko (who, a few years ago, passed away in

Tak Gyeong-hyeon

Tokyo). Living a closed and limited life, the young Korean pilot considered Tome as his mother and Reiko as his sister.

After the war, Tome left a meaningful word about a Korean soldier. When she was asked if she remember any particular thing about the suicide squad, she answered, "I still remember a Korean soldier. His name was Mitsuyama Fumitaka(Tak Gyeong-hyeon). I had pity on him because I had never seen that anyone visited him." Then she took out a small basket on the shelf. The basket was filled with faded pictures. She picked up a picture and showed it.

There were two people: young Tome and a soldier with a field cap. The young soldier was Mitsuyama Fumitaka. Although other soldiers were high spirited, he was a quiet person and liked to be alone. Reiko said that he always called

Tome 'mom.' Reiko and Tome heard his last song of Arirang. Reiko reflected on the past. Young soldiers got together upstairs the day before they went out on the last mission. They knew they were going to die. Families of the soldiers came and stayed for the night before the squad left for its fatal mission. But only second lieutenant Tak was alone. His family did not come. So my mom and I consoled him. Even though he did not like talking in public, he started saying something to us.

"Mom, I do appreciate your kindness. I'm going to sing a song for you. It is a song of my mother land."

Arirang, Arirang, Arariyo
Crossing the passes of Arirang
If you leave me, sweetheart
You will be footsore within a mile.

As far as Reiko remembered, he sang this song three times. Arirang was a song of Korea. He shed tears while singing. Only then they realized that he was a Korean. For the first and the last time, he identified himself as a Korean with the song of Arirang. He sailed out off to Okinawa at 6:30 am. on May 11, 1945. It was drizzling. His last moments are not known. The signal corpsmen in the airfield of Chiran were nervous. The communication facility was set up in the leader's fighter only. If the leader's fighter was shot and knocked out of the sky, there was no way to know about the other fighters. The signal was disconnected at 9:15 am, and all 36 soldiers did not come back.

He died only three months before the war ended. Why did he volunteer for the suicide squad? Shimahara, tried to figure out the history of second lieutenant Tak and what he might be thinking. "I'm going to die anyway. I would like to devote myself to my family. Mom can live better if I die in the battlefield."

It was true that the suicide squads who died in the war were respected as gods of war in Japan. As he experienced the discrimination against Koreans, he might have thought that he could save his family from the discrimination by dying for Japan. In August 1984, one Japanese tried setting up a monument to pay tribute to the memory of second lieutenant Tak. According to the plan, Tak's full name was to be on the front, and "Japanese captain and Arirang Kamikaze pilot Tak Gyeong-hyeon" was to be on the back. However, this monument has never been put up because a Korean newspaper criticized that the monument glorified Kamikaze.

It is true that Tak was a victim of Korean modern history. I strongly believe he should be recorded in the history of Korea. Other than that, a Japanese actress, Kuroda Hukumi, plans to raise a monument to the memory of the Young Korean squad who died in World War II. She said in an interview, "I hope this monument promotes friendship between Korea and Japan." However, due to some unexpected problems, her plan failed.

There is another story of the suicide squad. Kim Sang-pil, a first lieutenant had a story related to the song of Arirang. Kim graduated from Tachiarai Educational College in March 1944, and then was assigned to the pilot training troops. One day, the troops held a banquet. "I come from Joseon. Even though my Japanese is not perfect, I am going to sing a Japanese song." Then someone in the audience said "Please sing the song of Arirang. Sing for us."

"All right, I'm going to sing the song in Korean."

Arirang, Arirang, Arariyo.
I am crossing over Arirang hill
The one who abandoned me
Will not walk even ten ri before the feet hurt.

Arirang, Arirang, Arariyo⋯
I am crossing over Arirang hill
Just as there are many stars in the clear sky.
There are also many dreams in our heart.

Arirang, Arirang, Arariyo⋯
I am crossing over Arirang pass
There, over there that mountain is Baekdusan.
Where, even in the middle of winter days, flowers bloom.

In spite of the sad and depressed mood, they clapped their

hands at his song. Then, the song of Arirang was known to young Japanese soldiers. Arirang was the last song through which soldiers could understand one another. Arirang took them to their hometowns, their mothers and their countries. On April 3, 1945, he died in the battle and could not sing the song of Arirang again. Today, a monument stands in Memorial House of Chiran Airfield: "Sound of the song of Arirang fading away / Sakura fell missing the mother country."

Finally, we can not leave out Takayama Noboru. Before heading to the battle field he said clearly "why we have to die for the Japanese Emperor, it is nonsense!" Then he ended up his life on the front line.

Some of the suicide-squad members are still alive. Jo Jin-ho, a former Kamikaze member described their feelings based on his experience in the war :

First, curse on God for taking their lives
Second, hatred of mother country
Third, dread of death
Fourth, vanity of life

Yun Dong-ju, who is one of the famous Korean poets, sang the song of Arirang with his Japanese friends at the last meeting before he was arrested and finally died in a jail. As we have seen, in the 1940s, the song of Arirang had already become widely known to Japanese.

gg. Arirang and Korean Comfort Women in Southeast Asia during World War II

One can see the profound impact of Arirang on many Koreans who involuntarily served in the Japanese military during World War II. Women who served in the Japanese military brothels were called comfort women during the war time. Historians estimate that these comfort women numbered between 10,000 and 200,000. Although this number included Japanese women, the majority were Korean. They were recruited by coercion and deception to serve as sex slaves for Japanese troops.

I would like to approach this subject from documentary, historical, and personal perspectives. There have been reported many incidents on how Japanese troops abused Korean comfort women at the war front during World War II.

– The Incidents of Korean Women Slaughtered at Burma War Front

In 1996, a Japanese monthly magazine(*Bungeishunshu*) published an article by Sawazi Hosoe describing the death of Korean comfort women at the battle in Myitkyina, Myanmar. According to Sawazi, the Allied Forces(English and Chinese) killed some 1500 Japanese soldiers on September 14, 1944. Before Allied soldiers destroyed all the Japanese soldiers, however, the Japanese commander ordered his men to kill the Korean comfort women. It was an attempt to cover up what the Japanese military did to innocent Korean women. I arrived in Myanmar on 13 May 2012 to conduct field work on the Myitkyina area but unable to get permission due to security problem.

-The Story of Noh Su-bok in Thailand

Noh Su-bok is one of the Korean comfort women who survived her ordeal as a sex slave in Thailand in 1945. After the war ended, she got married and lived in Thailand concealing her sad story to the rest of the world. Almost forty years later, in 1984, she returned to Korea and told her story. According to Noh, Japanese recruiters promised her a well-paid job. When she arrived in Singapore in 1937, however, she was forced to become a sex slave for the Japanese soldiers there. Korean comfort women in Thailand, including Noh, had to sing for entertainment of the Japanese soldiers. One of the most popular songs they sang was "Arirang." Noh recalled how much the Korean folksong soothed her anguish throughout her nightmare in Japanese camps and her hard life in Thailand.

Noh's story illustrates how Arirang served as a spiritual song for Korean comfort women by providing hope and courage during those horrifying days. At an Arirang conference, a Korean poet Go Eun painfully portrayed Noh and her Arirang story when he said, "Arirang is song of the oppressed."

- Korean Women and Men in Okinawa during World War II

In 1991, Park Su-nam made a controversial documentary film entitled *Arirang-Testimony from Okinawa*. This documentary uncovered the inhumane treatment and sufferings of Koreans who were forced into service and sent to Okinawa. Specifically, the film focused on the stories of *Korean comfort women and conscripted Korean soldiers in Okinawa* during World War II. The film director painfully portrays the sorrow and agony these unfortunate Koreans experienced before they died. The film vividly describes the cruelty of the GGJ, and to remember the horrors wrought by war. It's our duty to prevent such atrocities from occurring in the future. Recently, remembering this tragedy has become more important as the current GGJ insists that the GGJ did not play any role in recruiting Korean comfort women during the war.

Park Su-nam was born in Kuwana, Mie Prefecture in Japan. He was a second generation Korean resident in Japan. While he worked for a publishing company, he decided to make a film on the Hiroshima bombing. The move was entitled *Song of Arirang, Another Hiroshima*. I was reminded of Park's theme when I attended a conference of the International Society of Geography at Okinawa in 2001.

One of the participants, Professor Hokama Shugen of Hosei University, fought against American soldiers in Okinawa as a young soldier. He told me that he personally witnessed the hardships of Korean comfort women and conscripted Korean soldiers there. It is important to note that this Japanese scholar admits how inhumanely the Japanese military treated Koreans during the war. Professor Hokama is one of the leading scholar of Okinawa Studies. I personally respect him very much in both academic excellence and warm personality.

hh. Itsuki's Lullaby and Arirang

Itsuki's Lullaby of Japan is sung around Itsuki(five trees) village in Kuma, Kumamoto Prefecture in Japan. The village is located about 25km away from Kuma downtown. The village is at the foot of a valley on the way to Kokanosho where the remnants of Heyke migrated to. The Itsuki Lullaby is particularly well known for its sorrowful melody and lyrics. It is also famous for submission and passiveness. Another lullaby of the nearby Hakada region, Kuju is opposite to the Itsuki's Lullaby. The lullaby of Hakada is characterized by the defiance toward masters who hired baby sitters.

Lately, the Itsuki's Lullaby was discussed for the relationship with Arirang of Korean folksong. Itsuki was named because there were standing five aged trees in the depth of mountains. The village is still a typical remote mountain hamlet with a population of about two thousands residents. It is very similar to Jeongseon in Gangwon-do Province, Korea.

The Itsuki's Lullaby is very unique in that the rhythm is triple time. Typical Japanese folksong are composed of 2/2 time rhythm. In 1930 Tanabe Ryutaro who was an elementary school teacher of the city made the musical score of the lullaby. Tanabe commented that "Since around 1935, this folksong lullaby had been broadcast through NHK in Kumamoto. I assume that the Itsuki's Lullaby has been sung by penurious women at the end of the Edo era. Therefore the lullaby was a song of woe, and became a representative song.

Kondo Ayako, a music teacher of a middle school in Hokkaido, Japan mentioned her thoughts about Itsuki's song as the follows :

Itsuki's Lullaby is very unique among Japanese songs because it is formed triple time. Japanese songs usually consist of binary time. The Korean folksong 'Arirang' is consisted of triple time. I have been curious about the difference between Japanese and Korean songs because those two countries are very close to each other geographically and historically in many ways. Therefore, I completely accede that the region of Kyushu, Kumamoto has the folksong formed with the triple time because of the Korean influence.

About four hundred years ago, there were huge construction projects in this area. At that time, the laborers were Korean captives who were caught during the Japanese invasion of Korea in 1592. Some of them stayed there after the construction was finished. A few stonemasons or engineers left for somewhere. As the Korean captives lived there, other Japanese residents became accustomed to the song of triple time rhythm. Almost 80% of Korean folksongs are formed with triple time rhythm. Why are most of the folksongs of triple time rhythm found in this area of Kuma? We need to look closer. Let me compare lyrics of the Arirang with one of Itsuki's Lullaby.

"If I die, who will cry for me?"

"A cicada on the pine trees might cry in the mountains."

This lyric comes up on Miryang Arirang. If you listen to both songs by turns, you will realize that these two songs are very similar. In order to understand Itsuki's Lullaby fully, you need to pay attention to the notion of lullaby. Generally, people regard the lullaby as the song to put a child to bed. However, once you listen to the song, you will not consider Itsuki's song as a simple cradle song. The Itsuki's song is not only a song for a baby but also an adult song of hard-luck. Therefore the song is both a lullaby and a tale of woe. Such a dual function can be found out from the folksong of Jejudo Island in Korea.

The Itsuki's Lullaby is an exception to Japanese lullabies, out of about eight hundred eleven lullabies. Many Japanese people do not know the meaning of the lyrics. Fortunately, Tosaka Yoshiko who came from this town knew the song well. At present, the Itsuki's Lullaby is recognized as Itsuki's Lullaby being based upon the song of Tosaka Yoshiko's lullaby in 1960. At present, the Itsuki's Lullaby is recognized as Itsuki's

Lullaby upon the song of Tosaka Yoshiko's Lullaby.

"I am waiting for Chuseok Chuseok Chuseok (Korean Thanksgiving day)."

"I would go home if Chuseok comes soon."

"I am Kanjin, Kanjin."

"They are high social position."

"Person of high standing."

"Wearing a luxurious belt and clothes."

People think that 'Kanjin' are Korean people settled in Japan since the 19th century. The residents in this town were Koreans. Additionally, the 14th descendant of a famous porcelain maker Shin Chukang who was taken to Japan during the Japanese invasion in the 1600s talked on a TV show as below:

"When I heard this song for the first time, I knew intuitively that the word Kanjin means Korean. However it is just my intuition, no reason. And I still think so."

Like he said, the triple time rhythm is very unusual historically and geographically in Japan. Also, the part of "Arorong, Arorong, Arongbai" is regarded as a flat of "Arirang Arirang Arariyo." And the part of 'Bi' is regarded as 'Yo.' Certainly there is some relationship between Arirang and Itsuki's Lullaby upon comparison with the similarity of refrain. In 1994, Gil Ok-yun who was a famous composer of Korea, said on a broadcasting in Japan that "Itsuki's Lullaby must be the song of Korea."

There are a plenty of opinions on when people began to sing the song. None of them is certain. One thing is true: people of Itsuki do not feel a sense of incompatibility with triple time melody. "Probably, the nostalgic song 'Arirang' was transformed into the cradle song 'Itsuki's song.'" Anyhow according to the melody, the song was sung for the soul of Koreans. Pema Gyalpo who is a Professor of Kihu University in Japan stated about feeling of Itsuki's Lullaby: When I listened to the song through my honored teacher, Kuramae Morimichi at the banquet, I was imbued with the spirit of the words rather than each word.

Generally, the folksong expresses the common people's feeling. Then it is persuasive that there is a similarity between Arirang and Itsuki's Lullaby. In 1957, Matsunaga Koichi stated about Itsuki's Lullaby on the Journal *Chuokoro*n in Japan. "The song of Itsuki's Lullaby is very beautiful and induces sadness in my mind. I was thinking where the sentiment of sadness came from. It is impossible that the sentiment came from just one person's emotion. I assume that the sorrowful feeling would bring up some sort of social formation."

One day he went to Itsuki, Kumamoto. Only 1% of village was cultivated land, and the rest of territory consisted of mountain areas and valleys. People would rather crawl than walk on the ground. Even though dwellers of Itsuki gave birth, people could not raise their baby well. Therefore if the baby, especially a girl, grew to be six or seven years old, the parents sent their child to another province as a baby sitter. The children accepted it to save food for their families and to be good children. The children sang the Itsuki's Lullaby at work where they missed home or mourned their pitiful circumstances. So they found the song of Itsuki's Lullaby was full of love and hate. The Itsuki's song was written with graceful words.

"What kinds of flower?"

"A Camellia."

"Water comes from the heaven."

Although people sing the song, they could not realize the profound meaning and thought. People who sang the song were ignorant about why the speaker compared life with camellia and why they said water came from the heaven. They just sang the song without seeking the deep thought in the lyrics. According to Matsunaga, the idea of 'Getting water from the heaven' would not be found in foreign songs. The expression stands on a high level literately and also moderated poetry may be unable to create the fine expression.

A writer Mosu said that the lullaby was written to reveal the social absurdities. Also the song has passed the way of Bohemian generations. He assumes that the lullaby included some mysteries. As for rhetoric, he thought that song was created roughly. He imagined that a professional poet passed beautiful words on to others. He viewed that the song flew like fluff and landed somewhere else, then from there it continued on flying and landing on people's mind as they keep singing the song.

Furthermore, the song contained the tragedy brought by the resistance of farmers who were deprived of all the cultivated land. Consequently, the opinion of Mosu seems to reveal the tragic history: Korean captives escaped to a remote and secluded place in the mountains 'Itsuki' to shun the discrimination and pressure by Japanese. In other words, the Koreans seem to have sung publicly about the hidden sorrowful history under Japanese pressure.

Most Japanese lullabies are binary time. Among them 811 lullabies, only thirty lullabies are triple time. Among the thirty, twenty four are found around Itsuki village in Kuma-gun, Kumamoto Prefecture. The Wuzu Drum Dance song and the Gokaso Kureko Dance song of Kuma are also triple time. According to the research by Murakami Masamichi, the triple time songs are found mainly in Southeastern Siberia, Mongolia, and Korea. Not surprisingly, Itsuki's Lullaby is triple time. Murakami thought that the triple time songs in Japan were carried into Japan by horse-riding people of East Asia.

It is worth noting that triple time songs are found mostly in Kuma region. During the Japanese Invasion in the 16th century, Kato Kiyomasa, the Feudal Lord of Kumamoto Prefecture took over ten thousand Korean captives to his country. I suspect the distribution of triple time songs is closely related to the incident. Murakami's view that the captives sang their homesickness and sorrow and it became Itsuki's Lullaby makes good sense. In my opinion, the Itsuki's Lullaby has a relation to Arirang in many ways. Alone this line further study is essential to clarify the picture of the Itsuki's Lullaby.

ii. Kusano Taeko and Arirang

In 1983-1984, I served as a visiting Professor in the Department of the Regional Studies at the Tsukuba University in Ibaragi Prefecture in Japan. At that time faculty members stayed in an apartment allocated by the university authorities in the rural area. However, on the weekends, most of Japanese faculty members went back to Tokyo to meet their family members.

Also, every weekend I visited Tokyo downtown with my wife for a change of air from monotonous Tsukuba life. Whenever we stopped by bookstores in Tokyo, we saw many books on the Koreans who migrated into Japan. From early four Kingdom period such as Silla, Goguryeo, Baekje and Gaya, Japanese scholars called Korean immigrants as *Kikajin* (naturalized person) but recently they named the Koreans as *Toraijin* (person crossing over to Japan). On the change of terminology from *Kikajin* to *Toraijin*, I have a different view then I used to adopt regarding the terminology about migrants. Consequently, Korean migrants moved into ancient Japan. They had unique contribution to the formation of ancient Japanese culture. I needed more time for research.

Therefore almost every year, I went to Japan to conduct field work. And I lectured at the Kyoto University and Ritsumeikan University. From this research I had a great deal of data and materials collected. In 1994 and I went to Japan again to collect data of Korean migration. I stayed at Kyoto University Guest House while I gave a lecture at the graduate school of Kyoto University. During that time I frequently visited bookstores located near the Kyoto Railway Station. By accident, I found a book entitled *Nippon no oto* (Sound of Japan) by Koizumi Humio. I was very interested in the diffusion of Japanese music in ancient Japan. I was keen on learning how he described the matter. I pulled the book out and opened it to the section on court music. He said clearly that the court music in Japan came from Korea. I bought the book and brought it with me to the US.

One day in May 2005, I was writing columns for the *Korean Times of Utah* about the song of Arirang. So in order to find out some more interesting stories, I pulled out Koizumi's book. Then, I carefully examined the text. Part I: Japanese music in the world, Part II: Japanese music today and tomorrow, Part III: Traditional music in Japanese culture, Part IV: the Orient and the Occident (East and West) etc.

After I read these chapters I was impressed to find out some of the sentiments toward Asian culture. Koizumi well described his view of the racial music in Asia and other racial music. Especially in his book he gave me significant knowledge to grasp the reality of folksong with reference to the universality of the folksong such as Arirang.

While I was collecting data relating to Japanese sources, I had by chance come back a book entitled *Arirang-Search for the Attraction of the Traditional Music in Korea* by Kusano Taeko. I immediately contacted the Kinokuniya bookstore in San Francisco. But I was disappointed to hear that they could not find the book. So book may have been out of print. However, I obtained the book in Korea. I was surprised to learn she was one of the best students of Koizumi Humio. She had a relationship with the song of Arirang, too.

She published her article *The racial music in Asia and feature of the traditional music in Korea* in *Korean culture* in April 1981. It was also published in the quarterly publication *Samcheolli* (March 1984). She is now teaching music at the University. While reading her book, I was impressed that she wrote that "there are people, there is a folksong." So Korea is the treasure house of folksongs and she picked up the song of Arirang as the core of the research. Despite the numerous folksong in Korea, she particularly selected the song of Arirang as the main theme. Kusano Taeko pointed out the following unique characteristics of the song of Arirang :

① Professional singers sing the song of Arirang.
② Whenever people get together, they willingly sing the song of Arirang.

③ Famous singers sing the song of Arirang as one of the essential repertoires.

④ Elderly women sing the song of Arirang while doing household chores.

⑤ The song of Arirang appears in the elementary school textbook. Children learn the song of Arirang.

⑥ Everybody knows the song of Arirang.

⑦ The song of Arirang is living in people's minds in various forms.

Throughout these elements, we may distinguish the song of Arirang from other folksongs. She said if we examined the song of Arirang in each region, we grasped the changes of folksong in Korea. To find the changing process of the origin or history of the folksong is to lead us to an understanding of the history of the common people. Kusano had a chance to listen to the song of Arirang. She felt a unique impression. "In fresh air, the song of Arirang accompanied by an hourglass-shaped drum is one of the best music in the world."

The origin of Arirang goes back to the past one thousand and several hundred years ago. Chinese music had an influence due to the geographical location, particularly of Central Asian countries bordering Western Regions of China. Also, she indicates the folksongs of Japan and Korea have some sort of similarity in the mode.

Also, interestingly enough, she touched on the Samullori's

history, and highly praised Kim Duk-soo, Choi Jong-sil, Kim Yong-bae and Lee Gwang-su. She fully understood the contemptuos treatment of Namsadang (wandering entertainment group) in Korean society, especially during the Joseon Dynasty. She respected their efforts to promote this type of show up to the modern society.

She sensed the melody of Jeongseon Arirang which reflected the feature of Gaeseong region and the influence of Buddhist music. Particulary she pointed out that the diffusion of the folksong in Korea owed much to the peddlers. This was a meaningful and productive suggestion in the study of folksongs in Korea. She also mentioned about the Gyeonggi Arirang, Gin Arirang of Gangwon-do, most of which were for the wives and friends of the peddlers.

In short, examined the book pointed out the root of traditional music, how to handle the song of Arirang, and Arirang as an Asian folk's music. Through this research she clearly delineated the characteristics of Arirang in Korea, especially noting the fascinating melody of Arirang.

As a follower of the late Koizumi Humio and professional musician, she treated resourcefully and objectively the folksong of Arirang based upon plentiful data and field work. She well described the book widely read by Korea people as well as Japanese people who loved the song of Arirang.

jj. Miyatsuka Toshio

Miyatsuka Toshio was first introduced the song of Arirang in the summer of 1973. While he studied at Kyung Hee University, Seoul, he and his friends visited a remote place called at Unnam-ri Gwirae-myeon, Wonju, Gangwon-do Province. After working all day in the field, they went to a small river to wash themselves. He said he couldn't forget the many a killifish in the small river.

After World War II, when he visited this village for the first time, the people were not friendly to him. He was Japanese and, he could not speak Korean. There was no way to communicate with the villagers. But one day he sang the song of Arirang, which he learned in Japan, with all his might, and the village people became friendly and the relationship went smoothly. Whenever the chance arose, he sang the song of Arirang. He realized that there were lots of variations of Arirang. Then he learned that each city or region has its typical tone of Arirang.

Primarily, his goal of studying in Korea was not the song of Arirang. He focused on the study of the shifting cultivation in Gangwon-do Province. However, he became enamored of Arirang while in Korea. If there were Korean people, there was the song of Arirang, just like National Anthem. Whenever they go, the song of Arirang is right there. The song of Arirang was sung by the Koreans who lost their motherland to Japanese occupation. They sang the song to soothe their sorrowful feeling. After the failure of the March 1st Independent Movement in 1919, Koreans were filled with pent-up anger. Singing of the song of Arirang gave vent to this.

Miyatsuka clearly indicated that he is not a professional musician, however there was a reason why he wrote about the Korean folksong Arirang: all Koreans and people of the world who understand the song of Arirang are driven into a fascinatingly charming world. Why do Korean people so deeply love Arirang? Why have so many people tried to analyze the song of Arirang for such a long time? The song of Arirang was sung at different times and regions by different races. Arirang was always in the hearts of people and was loved by the people. During the Japanese occupation, the GGJ attempted to ban the song of Arirang. Furthermore, they banned buying and selling the music records which contained Arirang, and confiscated the music records. They used every means to stamp out the song of Arirang. Even though the pressure was stronger and tougher, the song of Arirang was spread further and wider day by day all over the Korea.

According to Miyatsuka's book, broadcasting and drama on Arirang soaked the song into common people's life. Also Arirang crossed over the boundary of other countries. He also continued his field work with reference to Arirang which survived in North Hokkaido and Okinawa, Japan; South and North Korea; Yanbian, China; The Dumangang River and Mt. Baekdusan. Also in each area he met a great pressure of Arirang.

In 1990, he visited again Jeongseon, Gangwon-do Province and Miryang, Gyeongsangnam-do Province where are the birthplaces of Arirang. There he met Park Min-Il, who obtained his degree in the study of Arirang. I first met Park in 2007 in his house in Chuncheon, Gangwon-do Province. He was gentle and friendly, and has a warm personality. Miyatsuka described admiringly his personality. He described how he first met Park and was impressed by what impressed me. Park is an authority on the study of Arirang in Korea, but is humble and amicable.

Looking back, I was vey impressed by their conversation between Park, and Miyatsuka said "I can not read the score." Park said "When we sing the song of Arirang, we don't care. We did not know how to read the score, either. However anybody can sing the song of Arirang by heart. Each has his or her own melody of Arirang. They don't need any specific theory or argument. Consequently, the most important thing is why people sang the song of Arirang. Park said "Along this line, let us collect data as much as we can for the study of the song of Arirang."

In the end, they spent 4 hours in discussion. Then they came to the conclusion that Arirang is not about giving up but about overcoming hardships for a better future. Arirang was sung everyday regardless of occupation, gender, age and nationality. Also, they agreed that Arirang is one of the best folksongs to present to the world without hesitation. The conversation between them was graceful, meaningful and productive.

Miyatsuka briefly presented what chapters should be in his book.

Chapter 1 : The birth of the song of Arirang

Chapter 2 : Arirang crosses over the Joseon straight

Chapter 3 : The origin of Arirang and its puzzle

Chapter 4 : Visit to the hometown of the song of Arirang

Chapter 5 : Na Un-gyu and film Arirang

After I read his book, I felt that Miyatsuka had profound knowledge about the Korean culture, especially Korean history. Kusano's study of Arirang was examined from a professional and traditional angle. Miyatsuka's approach focused on the socio-economic history in Korea. This approach definitely gave the tremendous stimulus toward the study of Arirang in Korea. In this study he dug out great materials in Japan to update the information on Arirang in Japan. His publication will significantly contribute to understanding of the Korean culture among Japanese. Also, it will be an invaluable source of the study on Arirang in Korea.

b. China

According to the official data, the number of Korean resident in China amounts to 1,900,000, the largest in the overseas Korean population.

Most of them are Joseon group from Hamgyeong-do and Pyeongan-do Provinces. They have experienced a bitter life because of the political change of China and also struggled under the Japanese occupation before the liberation in 1945. The following lyric describes Korean life at the time.

New Arirang of Mt. Jangbaeksan

The sun is rising at the peak of Jangbaek Mountain Range and
The blue sea is waving boasting the blue wave and various
sceneries
Cheonji Fall with beautiful rainbow
Is decorating this country beautiful
Ari arirang seuri seuri rang ariari seuriseuri
Arari is in.
Jangbaek Mountain Range is our pride
Lalalala.

Long time ago fairies came down to Cheonji Fall
Today friends are coming to this village
Our Jangbaek Mountain Range blooming the flower of friendship
Is the fame of the country and the pride of Yanbian
Ari arirang seuri seuri rang ariari seuriseuri
Arari is in
Jangbaek Mountain Range is our pride
Lalalala.

Jangbaek Mountain Range is our pride
Lalalala.

aa. The Song of Arirang Sung by Koreans in Manchuria

After 1907, the number of Korean migrants into Manchuria rapidly increased. At that time Korea and China had an unsolved dispute relating to Jiandao. During this period, the GGJ set up a branch office at Jiandao, and declared it as Korean territory. Eventually it was announced that Jiandao belonged to China as a result of the negotiation between China and Japan. Regardless of this, the Korean migration continued. From 1907 to the annexation of Korea, about 10,000 Koreans migrated into the Jiandao area.

After the annexation of Korea, about 20,000 Korean people migrated and then in 1912 about 40,000 Koreans moved to Jiandao. Most of Koreans migrated due to poverty or for political reasons. Their national consciousness was very strong. Thus, Jiandao became the base for the independence movement against the Japanese, especially since the March 1st Independence Movement of Korea in 1919. After this movement, the number of exiles increased, most of them to the Jiandao, which served as the stronghold of the anti-Japanese movement. Also, they were always singing the song of Arirang in order to maintain anti-Japanese spirit.

bb. Singing the Song of Arirang while Leading Japanese Military into a Trap

Recently, Hwang Yu-bok, an instructor of Chungang Minjok Hagwon, published the data on the battles by the Anti-Japanese Korean troops under the name of *The Song of Arirang Resound in the Jungle*. This describes a sad story about the Korean people's life in Manchuria.

During the 1920's, Korean migrants muddled through the bitterness of life. They had to support the Korean troops at night time. During the day, they had to face the punitive force and nasty conduct of the pro-Japanese profiteers. It was exactly the same situation during the Korean War. The people living around Mt. Jirisan had the same experience. During the day, the innocent people had to serve the Korean Regular Army and at the night they had to face the communist partisans who hid in the forest of Mt. Jirisan. Under the circumstance, Korean migrants in Manchuria and the anti-Japanese Korean forces needed some sort of passwords to communicate confidentially. The song of Arirang was adopted as the signal between the Korean migrants and Korean guerillas.

One of the Korean residents prepared food to serve the Korean guerillas. However, a pro-Japanese Korean spy relayed this to the Japanese troops. The Kanto Military rushed into the Korean resident's house. The Japanese soldiers suspected that the prepared food must be for serving the Korean guerillas. Finally the military found the evidence that this house served and helped the Korean agents secretly. The old man, the house master, was asked, "Tell us where the hideout of Korean guerillas are. Tell us the location. Otherwise we will kill you and all your family!" The old man thought a short while, then told them, "Please wait. I will change my clothes." He put on new white clothes and then began to walk. Japanese soldiers followed him. The old man stopped on the pass. Then the old man began to sing the song of Arirang with a strong voice. Finally the Japanese realized the song of Arirang might be the signal. Thus the Japanese officer pulled out his sword and stabbed the old man. As he fell down on the ground, he was singing the song of Arirang :

Arirang, Arirang, Arariyo
Arirang seven passes closing over
(implying that there were seven Japanese soldiers behind him)

After a short time the Korean fighters heard the song and began to fire toward Japanese soldiers then wiped them out. The Korean soldiers ran up the pass and found out the old man lying on the ground. But it was too late. The old man died. The Koreans sang the song of Arirang all together for the old man.

In 2000, when I visited the Yanbian University by the invitation of President Park Mun-hwan, we had a chance to talk with Professor Kim Jong-hun, a leading figure of the locality. They said that Koreans in Manchuria should be reevaluated. They emphasized that Korean migrants in Manchuria should become a part of the history. From this conversation I learned that the Korean migrants survived such a hard time in Manchuria singing the song of Arirang. Light should be shed on the Korean migrants about their past and present to have clear picture of their history.

cc. Kim Koo and National Liberalization Army

In February 1896, Kim Koo killed a Japanese soldier Tsuchida at the tavern in Chihapo, Hwanghae-do Province. Due to this incident he was arrested and sent to prison. Later, by the pardon of Emperor Gojong, he became a free man. In 1898 he became a monk at the Magoksa Temple in Gongju, Chungcheongnam-do Province. In 1899, he quit the priesthood and converted to Christianity. Thus, he taught young people as a teacher.

In 1909, Ito Hirobumi Resident-General of Korea was assassinated by Ahn Choong Kun. Kim Koo was involved in this event. He was also involved in with the attempt on assassination of Terauchi Masatake, the GGJ. Thus he spent 6 years in jail. After the March 1st Independence Movement, he was unable to stay in Korea and sought asylum in China, where he became a key member of the Korea's Provisional Government in Shanghai and also established the Handok Party in 1922. In 1932, he sent Lee Bong-chang to Japan to

Kim Koo. President of the Provisonal
Goverment of Korea in Shanghai.

assassinate the Emperor Hirohito, but failed. However to kill the Commander in General Chief, Shirakawa Yoshinori at the Hongkou Park in Shanghai, dispached Yoon Bong-gil. After the special arrangement of the President Jiang Jieshi of China, Kim Koo set up the Institute for military training.

Thus in 1940, he became the President of the Korea's Provisional Government in Shanghai and organized the National Liberalization Army to fight against the Japanese soldiers in China. They were preparing for the landing on Korea. They felt the need for a military song. They searched the folksong which contained the activeness and braveness. Finally, they selected the song of Arirang for potential army songs. They chose the melody of Miryang Arirang. Then Kim Koo decided the army song for the National Liberalization Army.

The song greatly contributed in the preparation for the landing in Korea, especially when the National Liberalization Army joined the British army in order to prepare for the landing operation for Korea. Also, they were ready to land in Korea singing the song of Arirang. However, Japan surrendered to the allies before the Korean troops landed in Korea.

c. Russia

aa. Koreans with the Song of Arirang

In 1937, Joseph V. Stalin carried out the Korean deportation. 180,000 Koreans were forced to move from Primorskiy to Tashkent in Uzbekistan.

Chirchiq Arirang

White birch which we planted here several decades ago
has grown up to a nice leafy tree and
Stands firmly in Chirchiq rich fields and
Become a resting place for farmers
Young girls picking cotton gather here for the rest.
They are merry for the rich fields.
Uzbek girls from Korea and
Many Uzbek girls with bunch hair sit and get the Dombra
How well they play the Dombra, Korean folksong, Arirang.

Who knows how fast the hands picking cotton!
The hands playing Dombra
Are moving like butterflies.
They are enjoying singing like working with Dombra
They are singing Arirang merrily.

Girls who enjoy dancing like singing

Are dancing with Arirang hand in hand
Arirang arirang Arariyo
Arirang which has passed the Arirang Hill
Become the melody of friendship in rich Chirchiq fields.

About 180,000 Korean people were living around the Primorskiy. They wanted to be called Korean rather than Kareiski. They began to settle there in 1860. Originally, they were farmers who had a hard life in Korea due to the Japanese colonial policy. Because of this situation, they moved into the Primorskiy to find a new life. There were political exiles among them as well. But in September 1937, Joseph V. Stalin enforced the Korean migration into Central Asia. His order was under the assumption that Korean people secretly communicated with the Kanto Japanese Military Corp.

The picture of the monument of the first settlement of Koreans' in Central Asia
Source: http://www.ohmynews.com/NWS_Web/View/at_pg.aspx?CNTN_CD=A0000380240

bb. Joseph V. Stalin's Distrust of Korean people

Recently, Clint Eastwood who produced the film Letters from Iwo Jima stated his view, "politicians killed innocent people by driving them away to the war front." As Stalin wanted to justify his political scheme, he drove away the Korean people into Central Asia.

However, Stalin's view was mistaken. Korean people in Primorskiy were exploited by the Japanese colonial policy through GGJ. As GGJ took their lands, they became landless farmers without land and could not live in their homeland. They left their homeland to cross over the Dumangang or Amnokgang River, and they finally arrived at the Primorskiy. They believed they would be free from the Japanese occupation.

Stalin assumed that if Russia fought with Japan, the Korean people would stand on Japan's side. Along this line, N. F. Bugai clearly indicated that Stalin's view was wrong and he added that the real motive was to handle the internal political power struggle. In this connection, Professer Kim German, director of the research center of Koreanology at Kazakhstan National University criticized Stalin's unsound view toward the Koreans.

cc. Stalin's Clean-up of Korean Intelligentsia

As examined above, the forced Korean migration into Central Asia was not suddenly implemented. It was carefully planned. One of the evidence, Stalin imprisoned all Korean intellectuals who lived in the Primorskiy to silence their criticism.

For example, a writer Jo Myeong-hee arrived in Vladivostok, where there were about 200,000 Korean people in 1920. They first set up the School of Youth during 1920-1930. The Koreans including Jo emphasized the importance of education and of the independence of Korea. Jo taught students and wrote a novel entitled *The Nakdonggang River*. But Russian authorities assumed that he was an activist and imprisoned him. A lange numer of Koreans died from dysentery in the jail. He left behind his wife and five-year-old daughter at the age of 44.

In 1988 allocated a space for Jo Myeong-hee's Memorial Hall in the 3rd floor of the Naboi Literature Museum in Tashkent Uzbekistan.

dd. Muddling through 6,000km force Korean Migration

In 1937, Stalin called the chief of the Home Affair Committee secretly to Kremlin and gave a task to him, forcing Koreans to migrate from the Primorskiy to Central Asia. Thus 180,000 Korean people had to move to Kazakhstan, Uzbekistan and Kirgizstan in Central Asia. He ordered that all Koreans should leave with food and daily necessities in a couple of days.

In November 13, 1937, eight train cars were ready to start. First, four cars were loaded with 5,565 people. The forced

Enforced Korean Migration Route from Primorskiy to Tashkent
source: The Times Atlas of World(six edition) plate 38

Korean migration was carried out from November to December in 1937. According to the Soviet census, the number of Koreans totaled 172,000. The Koreans who were moved to Central Asia in 1937 are now in their eighties.

Park Boris appeared in the KBS Program and talked about the running train. The Russian soldiers suddenly stopped the train and threw the people out. Also, people could not go to the restroom. It was impossible to have a shower or even wash a face either. This journey took 20 to days. Many got sick and they were taken off the train.

ee. Treatment of Korean People in Central Asia

The late Alexander Solzhenitsyn(1918-2008) blamed Joseph V. Stalin's brutality in his novel *Archipelago Gulag* for the forced Korean migration(G. S. Luzhkov was in charge of project). The following note appeared in an independence newspaper :

In September 1937, the USSR mobilized KGB, Russia's secret police. One morning several thousand Korean people were dumped into the freight train and passed through the semi-desert area to arrive at Kazakhstan and Uzbekistan.

To obtain a clear picture of the forced Korean migration into Central Asia, I suggest reading the following articles published in the *Goryeo Ilbo*. They are Kim Victoro's *Korean People in USSR*, Oh Sam-son's *The Walk on Foot Korean's Way in USSR* and Kim German's *By Special Train from the Far East*.

On festival days such as the harvest party in the region, the Korean people song Arirang in this country. For over 70 years they have sung the song. They learned Arirang through the shoulders from their grandparents. Through TV shows, we observed that while someone like Kim Nicolay(82) and Ju Tola(74) played drums or accordions, other people began to sing Arirang.

Arirang, Arirang, Arariyo
Arirang gogaero neomeoganda.
Nareul beorigo gasineun nimeun
Simnido motgaseo balbyeongnanda (Korean)

There were famous actors, writers and generals among the forced Korean migration in 1937. A famous actress Lee Hamdeok lived in Vladivostok. She married Tae Jang-chun (1911-1960), a great writer. Three days after their marriage they were included in the forced Korean migration. Tae Jang-chun has a close relationship with General Hong Beom-do. Tae wrote about General Hong's life with reference to Arirang. He also wrote the opera *Arirang*. Once, he served a representative in the city of Ushtobe, Kazakhstan.

During the period of Japanese occupation, a time of homelessness, the freedom fighters who sought to regain our nation left a clear imprint in our history. General Hong Beom-do was born in Yangdeok, Pyeonganbuk-do in 1868, and led a difficult early life as a farm hand, having lost his parents at an early age.

Starting in 1883, he served a long sentence at the Pyongyang Penitentiary, and spent the next ten years working at the Suan Paper Factory in Hwanghae-do Province and the Daedong Minting Factory. This was the time when the Japanese occupation of Korea had become blatant, and the fate of the nation and her people were placed on the cutting board.

General Hong Beom-do

Unable to stand by and watch while the fate of the nation was at stake, General Hong formed an anti-Japanese volunteer army called the Righteous Army and began to participate actively in conflicts against the Japanese.

The first battle of the self-equipped volunteer army led by General Hong was the Battle of Huchiryeong in early November 1907. The General led the volunteers to obliterate the Japanese soldiers who relentlessly pounced on and on.

Later, General Hong operated out of the Russian Far East and northern Manchuria, winning brilliant victories everywhere. In 1919, he formed the Korean Independence Army with approximately 400 soldiers and became the Commander-in-Chief. In August and October of 1919, he led his army to Korea and led victories against the Japanese occupational forces in Gapsan, Hyesan, Ganggye, Manpo, and Jaseong, and in June 1920, killed around 120 enemies at the Battle of Bongodong, in Wangqing, Jilin Province, China. In October, the Korean Independence Army won a great joint victory at the Battle of Qingshanli, in Helong, Jilin Province.

General Hong organized freedom armies on many

occasions and served as vice-captain. As Japanese armed espionage in the Russian Far East increased, the Communist organizations of the region asked General Hong Almaty for assistance. General Hong cooperated with the Red Army and became a terrorist to the Japanese invaders. As he continued his active fighting for independence in the Russian Far East. In Fall 1937, General Hong was exiled to Kazakhstan, in Central Asia, and lived the rest of his life. The statue of General Hong stands in front of Almaty Park to this day.

May, 4, 1989, Choi Seo-myeon(the director of the International Korean Research Center) visited the Korean society in Russia. After the trip he wrote an article in the *Sports Seoul*. Let me summarize his article as follows :

With all Korean people together, the Korean people in Russia went out for a field excursion. On the way to our destination, someone started to sing the song of Arirang, and then all Koreans sang the song of Arirang together. I thought that the song of Arirang binds Korean people together. Consequently, the song of Arirang didn't sound sad. It was a great marching song. I remembered Arirang was a military song. I hope that the song of Arirang in Russia would be a song of hope for the motherland, Korea.

As we examined in the previous parts, the life of Korean people in Central Asia was rough and tough. But it was not an end of their agony. There are new problems emerging. The new generations have a hard time recognizing their identity.

ff. Arirang Festival in Central Asia

It has been 70 years since Koreans migrated into Kazakhstan. From August 10 to 13 2007, Arirang Festival was held by the Korean Association, the Foundation of the Overseas Compatriots and Korean Theater. Arirang Festival was one of the splendid, large-scale festivals held in Kazakhstan. Through this Arirang Festival, the Koreans in Kazakhstan wanted to demonstrate Korean culture to Kazakhstan society. Arirang Festival demonstrated the excellence of Korean culture represented by the traditional folksong of Arirang indicating the joys and sadness of Korea life. Leena, a Russian lady(68) said "I was raised in a Korean village. Even though my face is different, I am used to Korean culture." She performed the Korean dance.

At the end of Arirang Festival, all Korean people began to sing the song of Arirang. Over 500 Korean people who came from various places sang the song. In spite of the barren soil, unfriendly climate, and wildness they survived and settled there for more than 100 years. But they never forgot the song of Arirang.

After the forced Korean migration into Kirgizstan, Kazakhstan, Uzbekistan, and Tajikistan, Turkmenistan in Central Asia, about 500,000 Korean sons and grandsons settled there.

The distribution of Korean people was acknowledged after the open-door policy of Mikhail Gorbachev. It was impossible to talk about the forced Korean migration until the open-door policy was implemented. In Kirgizstan various ethnic groups co-exist. And this country is called the Alps in Central Asia. Certainly, its physical setting is beautiful. Furthermore, there is less racial discrimination. Over 20,000 Korean people live in Kirgizstan. However, their lives are far from blessed. Especially, second generation Korean migrants are struggling with a hard life. To overcome the hardships, the senior citizen group 'Dongbaek' (Camellia) was organized. They are teaching Korean drums, dance and etiquette to the 3rd and 4th generations to hand down the Korean traditional culture. They enthusiastically teach their descendants to help them remember their roots.

The Dongbaek knows the song of Arirang. They learned the song from their fathers or grandfathers. They are longing for the motherland. Their hearts are filled with love and hate. They sing the song of Arirang in order to ease their sadness.

gg. Living Comfortably and Successfully in Tashkent by Rice Farming

Kim Pen Hva(Byeong-hwa) Kolkhoz is located 30km away from Tashkent, the capital city of Uzbekistan. The Kolkhoz was established by about 400 Koreans who moved here in

Korean farm practice at Kolkhoz in Tashkent

1937. When they had to move, they kept their farming instruments and rice seed with them. When they were left in the wilderness of Far East, they did not give up their life. On the contrary, they practiced cultivation in order to survive under the tough circumstance. They reclaimed the wasteland and started farming. The neighbors usually cultivated cotton, and they did not even know how to grow rice. The Korean Kolkhoz became one of the most successful Kolkhozes. Thus 'Kareiski' meaning 'Korean' once became a synonym with rich people at that time. The diligence of Koreans was their key factor of success.

At present, the Kolkhoz is still expanding the business abroad. Lee Riera(80) is one of the Korean residents in the Kolkhoz. She told the story of the deportation. "I was carried by a train for about one month. Many people died of malnutrition or diseases on the way. When we arrived here, there was no house. For the first time, we lived in a Yurt(a portable, felt-covered, wood lattice-framed dwelling structure used by nomads in the steppes of Central Asia)." Lee lives with her oldest son and the daughter-in-law with 13 grandchildren. She still eats kimchi and keeps kimchi in a jar. She says that the Koreans of Kolkhoz still stick to Korean culture. They continue to show Korean films in the theater, and perform the Korean traditional dance and music. Also, they learn the Korean language starting from the first grade in elementary school. After she finished her talk, she sang the song of Arirang in Korean, shedding tears.

hh. Field work in Chirchiq Korean Village in Tashkent, Uzbekistan

I was very keen to visit the Chirchiq, Tashkent, Uzbekistan and Almaty, Kazakhstan in order to obtain futher informations on the life of Korean people in Central Asia. Thus we left seoul, Korea for Tashkent.

We visited first the Korean Language School and met the person in charge for that school whose name is Ms. Kim Illina, 3rd generation Korean. She and the staff members were very kind enough and we discussed about our field work plan. Their suggestion were splendid so we decided to visit as following :

Korean Village in Chirchiq Area
Kim Pen Hva Muzeyi
Arirang Sanitarium
Korean Graveyard

Through this field survey, I wanted to learn their birth place (South or North Korea) in conjunction with the Korean deportation of September to November in 1937, and the situation of their life and the mindset for their origin, Korea.

During my field trip, I met a teacher of Korean Language School, Mrs. Lee A, and her husband who is pastor. She had 10 brothers originally when they had lived in Khabarovsk until 1937.

She was very knowledgeable, so I asked many questions through the conversation. Where is your birth place? For this question, she answered that most of people here don' t know where their birth place is. However, their voices and accents were not same as those of South Korean. I questioned that they were born from the North Korea. One of them said that her hometown is the Namwon, Jeollabuk-do Province, South Korea. This lady was the manage of the Kim Pen Hva Muzeyi. When she visited the Namwon in South Korea, everything has been changed so it was impossible to find anything those were kept in her mid.

We met one grandmother who was over seventy and lived with only his grand children. Her daughter-in-law was in Korea for earning money. This grand mother said that my parent used to say we were from Jinju in southern part of Korea but the place of forced to move was in Khabarovsk. When the mood was matured I asked them as usually I did. "Did your parent, mother or father used to sing the song of Arirang?" Yes, they were and we also follow them. Until now we used to sing the song of Arirang. I asked them for singing the song of Arirang all together. Eight of the people in the room sang together and suddenly a beautiful melody of Arirang was filled in the apartment.

Next we moved to the house and met Kim Iskrala at the age of sixty three years. There were her daughter-in-law and grand daughter who were the second and third generation. Every house we visited they invited their guest at the main room neglect of their house conditions and guest's opinion. For this reason we were planning to meet at their yard.

The weather of outside in Chirchiq's in October just looked like the beginning of the fall in Korea. We had dialoged seeing the pumpkins and fruits those were hanging on the trees. I could find their faces changed into sorrow when we were talking at the forced immigration. This lady also didn't know where she was from.

Korean village in Chirchiq

The house structures of this area when we visited from and there it was hardly to find the similarity of the Korean house style. Most of them were a simple house of Soviet style in a wild field. Endless of the story was linked we should depart the house and the grandma came out of their house for greeting and hugging, I felt a strange by seeing one of the house gate which made a concrete door who could not see inside the house.

When we came out of Kim Iskrala's house, I asked the driver who was waiting for us in the car, "I know that around here there is a Chirchiq River. Can we go there?" Regardless of

Chirchiq River sites one hour distance form Tashkent

my asking the driver moved his car for Chirchiq River. When I searched the literatures about the bitterness Korean in Central Asia, I could found the sad stories about them.

At last we arrived at the river and took out of the car. When I handled my camera on my hand and walked toward the bridge, Mrs. Kim also followed me. And she communicated : I heard from my parent that this river was made by the Koreans with weeding hoes and shovels and I saw tears of her face. There was a hydro electronic power plant on this vast and deep river. When we took the car, the driver mentioned that not only the Chirchiq River but also the Tashkent River was digging with the Koreans. And in addition he talked that the vast cotton field also made by the Koreans by getting rid of the weeds with shovels and hoes in the past seventy years.

When we drove toward Tashkent from Chirchiq, I catched one advocated the paper noted Arirang Nursing Home. Already the days were dark I asked my driver "Do you know how to go to this nursing home?" and then he said, "Yes, I could go." Thus we turned to the way on there.

When we arrived at the cleaning nursing home, the vice principal, Kim Lira showed her happy welcome and introduced those facilities and introduced the principal, Choi Sung-cheol. Later we entered the room gathered about 30 grand Mom and Papa. Every body looked healthy, we shared various issues and then we asked about the Arirang. Did you hear that your parent sang a song Arirang when you were children?" Most of them answered with loud voices, Yes I did and we also followed them. They also sang a song on Doraji and 'Home that I lived' too.

I introduced my self that I came here to hear of your song on Arirang. Do you mind to sing the song of Arirang? Then all of them were exited and I took the leader of the song and about 30 members of the nursing home were singing the song of Arirang.

Arirang Arirang Arariyo
Arirang gogaereul neomeoganda

International health care(Arirang Nursing Home)

Nareul beorigo gasineun nimeun
Simnido motgaseo balbyeongnanda.

We sang the song of Arirang again and again. I hold one of the grandpa who set beside me and song together. Because of their loud voice, the melody of Arirang filled out the nursing home with vitality.

It was a moment with full of deep emotion that was unexpected on my schedule. At that time one of the grandma said this was the rest time to move other place, but they wanted to stay hear to sharing. They looked like to see the people from outside. At that time I asked one of the granma who set across me so easy to eye contact; where were you from? She said "No." She seemed to come from the northern part of Korea as I hear her way of talking. Then I asked her age and she said she was 75 years old. As a reaction they asked me how old were you? So I said that I was 88 years old and then all of them were surprised that I came far from America and blessed with clap to be healthy.

It was short time but truly happy time to meet Korean grand mom and papa at the Arirang nursing home. We left the home with transmit by vice principal. Again we went toward the Tashkent blessing all of the grand mom and papa in good health and the nursing home were left behind in a dark places.

ii. Seeking for the graves of Koreans

It was the last day of our field trip on October 12, 2012 we were going to Seoul tonight at ten o'clock twenty minute by Asiana Airlines. In the morning we left the hotel to meet Ambassador Jun Dae-wan with sincerely and then seeking for the graves of Koreans in Chirchiq of Tashkent. They said we needed not to take a taxi for it was very near from hotel to the Embassy of Korea, I thought it was not polite with perspiration by waling but there were no other ways because of the language problems and difficult to take a taxi. So I decided to walk with my wife. It was a pleasant day for walking just like the weather of the fall in Korea. There were not crowed in the street so that we were happy to walk to the house of Korean Embassy.

It was crucial as usual as other countries to prove our identities at the gate of the Embassy but there was a ring from the secretary office of Ambassador and asked where were you from with fluently so I answered that I came from the University of Utah in Utah. At last the guider smiled and introduced us to the office of ambassador in politely. Therefore without any inspection we could come to the Ambassador's office.

I had no relationship with the Ambassador Jun only I knew him through his book *Do you know about Uzbekistan*. It must be very hard for him to write a book while he worked in his busy life as an Ambassador. I knew him only by his book. Without appointment I just to visit and left my name card but I could meet him because he was in the office. He was so kind and looked young even though he said he was over 60 years old.

We had greetings with joyfully and I told him about my visiting purpose for search the song of Arirang from Koreans in here, and looking for the monument of the General Hong Beom-do but we should leave tonight so we didn't have enough time to visit that places. As soon as he listened he stood up and copied the picture of the monument of the General Hong that searched in the computer and gave it to me. In addition, he said the important resource items were not only for the underground resources but also for the medical plants.

Seen the richness of the vast field and cool weather in the train for Samarkand, I could guess the words given by the Ambassador were important to keep in my memories. Ambassador Jun was an authority on the Russia for he has been worked at the beginning of the establishment of the Embassy in Primorskiy. We stood up and said him now we should go for the graves of the Koreans. We had farewell greetings with the Ambassador and out of his office. We were gotten out for search of Bektemir, Sergeli Region, Tashkent of Korean Graveyard. But we need taxi.

I remembered that the driver's daughter worked in this Embassy from the wife of the driver whom we were together for the field survey, so I asked the secretary of the Ambassador and a little later they asked me to wait a while. His daughter came to us and said her father would come here to bring us the graveyard. We got into the car there were his wife also thus we were together to a journey with them. And then she insisted us to invite for lunch at her home because of her daughter's opinion, and so took lunch with them regardless of our opinion. Her house located in a beautiful place near the house of president of Uzbekistan.

The driver said his son Jay also worked at the embassy of the US. After we had delicious food, then we sang the song of Arirang that was one of my habits. At last the driver learned the song of Arirang with his guitar and sang a song again and again until he was well playing this song. At last he could sing the

Korean new graveyard sites in the northern part of Tashkent.

song of Arirang accompanied with his guitar. What a precious time we had. Was it a merit of the song of Arirang easy to learn? We left the home behind the other song of Arirang.

When we arrived at the first grave, there were a hundred of grave stones in a vast of graves field. The grave stones were good quality of stones and large size but every grave stone they hang a picture of the dead parent. This was not the place that seeking by the author. In America, the graves of emigrants in the remote field of Midwest were looked poorness those were the workers in the mine who came back from Hawaii in 1930s. But all of the grave stones here were so big.

Korean old graveyard sites in the northern part of Tashkent.

When I met the Ambassador Jun at the Korean Embassy in Tashkent, he mentioned that recently they got funds from Korean Government and business sectors to the Association of Korea or Korean Groups so I thought that most of the Koreans were living in poor situation. Was it true even though they were poor they had enough money? For me it was hardly to believe that with out big money it would be impossible to construct these kinds of big monuments.

Asking the grave keeper, we visited the second Korean's grave. This place was the same size as we had seen at the first. I asked the grave keeper to show any grave those made with soils, and he signed to the driver to go to the other place. We were wondering here and there it was impossible to find the grave that I was longing to see in my mind.

At that time we met one lady with blue color plastic bag who was the cleaner of this grave. I asked her. Around of this grave yard was there any Korean or Siberian berried earlier? She thought a long time and then asked to follow her. We followed her without any word. She pointed one place with her hand. This was the grave that we were looking for. All of the information that indicated when they died or who were they only recognized that the male was from Korea and his family name was Chae, and his wife was Russian. This grave stone was berried on the land and poorness and a low. Probably this was the berried figure of the Koreans whom were forced to move. Desiring to see more I asked her to show another grave. She nodded her head and there were no more. Thus we came back to the hotel in Tashkent.

In the way back to the car I concerned the big monument of the Koreans in the grave yard. It was touched my mind that the future generation of the forced emigrated Koreans didn't use the money from the government for them and bought the land and stones for their ancestors who came to Tashkent from Primorskiy with all of their pains. This was the way of comfort for their mother and father's death to resolve their bitterness in the earth.

jj. The Ethnical Koreans of Central Asia

Last October 10, I was visiting Samarkand when I received the luck of participating in a church-organized meeting with ten elderly women. Most of them were second generation Ethnical Koreans, over 70 years of age. I shared many stories with them, and was able to ask them many things I had wondered about. The names of the women in the meeting are as follows :

Ju Clara, Kim Olia, Lee Vera, Kim Clara, Kim Tanya, Kim Galina, Lee Vanova

The answer to the question about Arirang, the folksong, is the same everywhere. They grew up surrounded by Arirang, and still sing it. Their hope is to visit Korea some day before they close their eyes. Many of them are originally from North Korea. They also wanted to wear the beautiful hanbok at least once, if possible.

For breakfast they eat Korean-style kimchi, bean sprouts, cheonggukjang, and white rice. In particular, on Hansik Day, a Korean traditional day, everyone gathers and holds ancestral rites.

Kazakhstan is a country with a very large territory. Most of the land are grasslands, and home to perhaps the largest number of the Ethnical Koreans in Central Asia. Kazakhstan was once occupied by the Mongols in the 13th century. That's why they have some Mongol blood. Kazakh people share the general characteristic of black hair, a round and wide face, and small eyes and ears. Their skin color is generally the same as that of the Mongoloid race. Were they to stand next to Korean people, it would be hard to discern them apart. They also have the Mongolian spot, as Koreans do.

The language of Kazakhstan belongs to the Ural-Altaic language group, and has the same syntax as Korean. The verb goes at the end of the sentence. They say that someone proficient in Korean can communicate reasonably in Kazakh after about 3 months of study.

The Ethnical Koreans, who were exiled there in 1937 forgot most of their Korean. However, their pride really touched me. They had forgotten their language, but they had not forgotten Korean traditional culture. They had kept the tradition of 'doljanchi' and 'gimjang', and were eating foods like kimchi, dried radish green broth, and rice cakes. Not to mention Arirang. They would sing our folksong Arirang every where they went, with parents and friends, so perhaps they could forget their Korean, but they could never forget Arirang.

The Ethnical Koreans were abandoned in Central Asia due to Stalin's inhumane measures. However, they are playing an important role in today's politics, industry, and economy. In Kazakhstan, the Ethnical Koreans play a crucial role for Korean businessmen to settle down in the field. Ethnical Koreans are also cooperating actively with foreign aid policies set by the Korean government.

In particular, Ethnical Koreans are stepping in when cultural obstacles are found in the progress of the works. Likewise with religion. Kazakhstan allows freedom of religion, so many religious workers are entering to proselytize. As priests or pastors from Korea start their ministry, they receive great help from the Ethnical Korean translators. While ministers from the US and Europe fail to start a church even after years of work, Koreans are carrying out their ministries relatively easily.

What I have felt in my visit is that in spite of the obstacles, the Ethnical Koreans are working faithfully and trustworthily in the five nations in Central Asia. This is a source of great pride for us, as well as a great blessing.

kk. Construction of Naboi Theater in Tashkent

After the Japanese surrendered in 1945, about 450 Japanese soldiers were captured and curried from Manchuria to Tashkent. In 1947, the Soviet Union was building the Naboi Theater in commemoration of the Revolution. The Theater was completed under the command of a Japanese captive, Nagata Yukio. When a strong earthquake hit the area of Tashkent in 1967, many buildings collapsed, but the Naboi Theater stood as it was. Even though Koreans and Japanese were moved forcibly to Tashkent as the victims of the war, the people of Tashkent are grateful to the Koreans and the Japanese for their contribution to Tashkent.

d. The United States and Europe
aa. Korean Adoptees in America and Europe

Arirang sung by immigrants to America or Europe is different as compared with that in other regions described before. The living conditions of America and Europe are more stable than those of other countries. However, living away from the homeland has a similar connection with Arirang as Koreans in non-Western countries.

One of the Korean students at the University of Utah encountered one American who sang Arirang when she finished her presentation of Arirang in her class. The elderly man was American and he could not speak Korean. The Korean student asked him "How do you know Arirang?" He said he has an elder sister adopted from Korea when she was four years old. My sister is half-Korean and half-American. Her father was American and her mother was Korean. Although she was not able to speak Korean, she used to sing a song in Korean. He learned the tune easily from her singing. Later, he found out that it was the song of Arirang.

Considering her age at the time of adoption and America as her living environment, it is remarkable that she was able to recite Arirang. Her classmate said that his sister was almost 50 years old. She has sung the song for more than 40 years and likely continues to sing it.

Jin Yong-seon who is an expert of the song of Arirang and principal of Jeongseon for Arirang School, has been to Holland in Europe. He searched evidence for Arirang in Europe and found one at a restaurant in Holland. There was a party for adopted Korean people at the restaurant. They shared their stories. And at the end of the party, they sang the song of Arirang. They could not speak Korean and have never learned it, but they sang the song of Arirang. Jin still wonders how they knew the song of Arirang living out of Korea and why they sang the song of Arirang.

I believe Arirang has a special touch on Korean people in the way they feel about their nationalty or loved ones. Adoption of many Korean children was brought out of the Korean War. It is such a sad history of Korea. The adopted kids may comfort themselves by relating them to Korea by singing Arirang in their adopted countries. In a way, Arirang connection may help them to reach to their biological parents hearts.

bb. Arirang at an Elementary School in the US

Kim Jeremy Yun-jae was born in France, and went to an elementary school in Korea as a first grader. And then he moved to America. He is good at English and Korean as well, and he is familiar with Korean culture and American culture. His father tries to help Jeremy remember Korea. Jeremy reads Korean books everyday and goes to Korean history class once a week.

One day Jeremy said to his father, "My friends and I are going to sing Arirang, the Korean traditional song in the school concert." In American schools, some American teachers teach Korean songs to their students. Such a trend suggests a popularity of Arirang and there seems to be no boundary in the world of music.

I had similar experiences with my own grandchildren. A few years ago, my granddaughter Arine Lee Seung-A played the violin on my birthday. Before she started, she said that "This is a song you like." Then the very familiar melody was coming out of her violin. It was Arirang. She was only nine years old and born in America. She has never been to Korea in her life. I wondered how she knew and played the song of Arirang. I thought that she got a lesson her how to play Arirang from her parents for my birthday. But she said that I taught it to her once by humming when she was 5 years old. She remembered the melody of Arirang she learned 4 years before. Her parents said they had never taught how to play the song of Arirang.

I would like to share the conversation with my youngest son in Washington D.C. During the conversation, he talked about his experience of Arirang in the US When my family migrated to the US in the 1970s, he was going to high school. He transferred to Hoover High School in Fresno, California from Korea. One day there was a competition of music performance among the Fresno School district California. Each team had practiced for the competition as hard as they could. After a little while, when one of the teams began their performance, he his ears.

"Isn't that the song of Arirang?" He said he could not believe that the high school students of America played the song of Arirang for their big event. In the 1970s, Korea did not open its gate yet, so there was little interchange with other countries. The main channel of cultural exchange between Korea and America was the Korean War.

I found a similar experience with my other grandsons in Saline, Michigan. In March 2001, my grandchildren, Dennis Lee and Jay Lee, played Arirang in the school band concert in Saline, Michigan. I regret missing their Arirang performance, but I was very fortunate to attend another grandson, Chris's Arirang performance at the same school in March 2008. It was an extraordinary experience to listen to Arirang music played by my own grandson.

My family story on Arirang suggests that many other orchestras and bands would have played Arirang in other parts of America and of the world.

Recently, the New York Philharmonic Orchestra performed in North Korea. It is a historic event. North Korea has been isolated from the world, and has kept the gate closed to others. The concert was broadcast live on radio and TV.

The repertoire included the beloved Korean folksong

'Arirang.' They chose the song of Arirang for the historic concert. Arirang was "Arirang Orchestra" which was arranged by Choi Song-hwan, musician of North Korea. Since he performed the Arirang Orchestra in 1976, it has been played in every official event such as June 15 Summit Meeting of both Koreas.

People's Love of Arirang

Chongseokjeong stands on the Gangwon-do Beach

8
Chapter

1. H. B. Hulbert

In 1886, linguist and historian H. B. Hulbert(1863-1949) whose Korean name is Halbo came to Korea by the invitation of Emperor Gojong. He taught English at the Yugyeong Institute and studied Korean history. In 1905, he published *History of Korea* and *The Passing of Korea*. He was the first foreigner who recorded the score of the song of Arirang. Additionally, he contributed in the field of politics when Korea was undergoing a very tough time.

He edited the *Korean Review*, in which his pioneering history in Korea was serialized(1901-1904). It was published in two volumes in 1905. Not only was he a friend of the Emperor of Korea and an outspoken champion for Korea independence, but he was also a royal emissary to Washington in 1905-1906 and to the Hague Peace Conference in 1906-1907.

After the enforcement of the Japanese protectorate over Korea, he was forced to leave Korea in 1906. He had a great affection for the Koreans. He mentioned, "Koreans are romantic, epic and instructive people." (Chosun Ilbo, October

The picture of H. B. Hulbert and Monument

30, 1985) In 1949, at the age of 86, he returned to Korea at the invitation of President Syngman Rhee. However, the strain of travel was too much for him and he passed away in Seoul on August 5, 1949, just one week after his arrival back in Korea. He was buried in Seoul Foreigners' Cemetery in Hapjeong-dong. The epitaph reads, "I would rather be buried in Korea than in Westminster Abbey" as he used to say.

The following is the preface to his book *The Passing of Korea* (1906):

Dedicated
To his Majesty

The Emperor of Korea

As a token of high esteem and a pledge of unwavering allegiance at a time when calumny has done its worst and Justice has suffered an eclipse And

To the Korean people

who are now witnessing the passing of old Korea

To give place to a new, when the spirit of the nation, quickened by the touch of fire, shall have proved that through "sleep is the image of death."

It is not death itself.

Korean Vocal Music

The musical score of the Arirang of Hulbert

2. Famous Folksong Singer Pete Seeger

In 1953, a famous folksong singer Pete Seeger visited Korea and sang the song of Arirang. During the 1960s, famous musicians such as Bob Dylan, Joan Baez, The Brothers Four, Peter Paul and Mary, and Pete Seeger were categorized as anti-war musicians. Pete recorded the song of Arirang and listed it as an anti-war song. Pete composed many anti-war songs such as "Where Have All the Flowers Gone?" and he encouraged young singers to sing anti-war songs. Pete Seeger was a noted folksong singer, composer, lyric writer and great master of anti-war music as well. Pete Seeger has an unique insight into the song of Arirang. He used to make a comment on the song before he started to play the song with the banjo.

Korean people sing a lot of songs. Among them there is the song of Arirang. It has been sung so many years. However, during the Japanese Occupation period the GGJ prohibited this song. I know South and North Korea are now fighting each other. Looks like they are totally different countries. But they,

Pete Seeger

South and North, all sing the song of Arirang. That means they are one country. Practically, they are separated, South and North, and surely they are fighting. But I think of Korea as one country. To sing the song of Arirang means they are the same people and one nation. Therefore, I assume that Korea will be united as one nation sooner or later.

In 2005, I had great pleasure to meet him in New York in order to invite him to Arirang Festival in Korea. He stressed that someone should work on sharing such a beautiful folksong with other peoples. He also explained that his poor health condition did not allow him to accept the invitation to Arirang

Festival in Korea. He wrote down the lyrics of the song of Arirang on the score on a piece of paper. This goes as follow:

Arirang, Arirang, Arariyo …
Crossing the passes of Arirang
If you leave me, sweetheart
You will be footsore within a mile

Arirang, Arirang, Arariyo …
Arirang, gogaero neomeo ganda
Nareul beorigo gasineun nimeun
Simnido motgaseo balbyeong nanda

Also, on the spot he wrote a short note for Koreans:

August 12, 2005
Dear Peace-loving people of Korea:

My wife and I are very sorry that we cannot come to your festival September 22-26. I sang the song 'Arirang' over fifty years ago. Now at age 86, I have little voice, but I sometimes sing it to myself. Music may help bring all the people of the world together.

Love to you all   Pete Seeger
Beacon, North New York 60 miles north of New York City

Pete Seeger's letter. indicating that a study of folksong is not easy but don't give up move forward…

I wrote Peter Seeger that I could use any information on Arirang, but he told me to proceed, since he had nothing useful for me. He then said that as I follow with my Arirang studies, I would face many obstacles, but I should not give up, and I should be strong and keep working hard. He sent me a letter, handwritten, not typed, declaring that neither the agricultural revolution nor the industrial revolution occurred in a short time span.

As he predicted, I faced many obstacles as I continued my works. Many times I wanted to give up, but I remembered his words and reminded myself that this was no easy path to take. I made up my mind to never back down, regardless of what may stand on my way, as Seeger had implored. I pledged to not step back regardless of the hardship I may face.

I hold in my heart the words from a master of the folksong as renew my strength and keep running, hoping to one day see the results of my work.

3. George Nasse and
Paul Vandermeer

In the middle of 1950 I spent a few years at the University of Michigan for my advance degree of Geography. I had two roommates: George Nasse and Paul Vandermeer. We resided at 1003 Packard Street, Ann Arbor. During this period George used to sing the folksong of Shenandoah. It is an American folksong. The song was beautiful. The melody in a sense was similar to the song of Arirang in Korea. So I always sang Shenandoah together with George. Certainly this Shenandoah soothed my homesickness. Just the melody was fascinating for me.

Now my oldest son's family lives in Saline near Ann Arbor, Michigan. So I occasionally visit them. I always visit 1003 Packard Street to recollect my old days and my friendship with George and Paul. However, sadly George passed away in the summer of 2006 in Fresno, California.

Shenandoah was regarded as the song of land. It is now deemed the song of river and the sea. In the summer of 2006, I visited my second son who lived in Fairfax, Virginia near Washington D.C. While I was staying there I visited the Library of Congress to find the date of the chant "Shenandoah". But I was unable to get the sources that I sought. Instead, I toured the Shenandoah Valley, Virginia. I enjoyed the beautiful natural environment and the legend related to Shenandoah.

Shenandoah was also considered as a love song. The text of the song tells a love story between a Native American girl and a white man, a fur collector. He was trying to take her out and then to cross over the Missouri River. I find a certain connection between Shenandoah and the song of Arirang.

Professor Lee Jae-wu at Mokpo National Maritime University wrote an article entitled "*Romantics during the age of sailing vessels and the song filled with love and hate.*" In this article he described the folksong Shenandoah as a folksong of America. It was sung by sailors. I was charmed by the melody of Shenandoah. In order to find out some sort of similarity between Shenandoah and Arirang, I am going to describe the following:

Arirang and Shenandoah share something. Today, if we raise a question "What is Arirang?" there will be many answers. There are hundreds of stories and theories. In this regard the Shenandoah has the same nature with Arirang. The two songs soothed down the sadness, isolation, and loneliness.

Oh Shenandoah, I long to hear you
Far away, you rolling river

Oh Shenandoah, I long to hear you
Away. I'm bound away
'Cross the wide Missouri.

Oh Shenandoah, I love your daughter
Far away, you rolling river
Oh Shenandoah, I love your daughter
Away. I'm bound away
'Cross the wide Missouri.

Oh Shenandoah, I'm bound to leave you
Far away, you rolling river
Oh Shenandoah, I'll not deceive you
Away. I'm bound away
'Cross the wide Missouri.

source : Songs of the World, Cho Hyo-im et. al, Taelim Publisher(2006)

Arirang in Korea, especially Jeongseon Arirang originated from the Auraji River. It is a love song between a girl and a boy. They exchanged whispers of love across the Auraji River. The water of the Auraji River was always dangerous. It was a serious obstacle. In summer if it rained heavily they needed the help of a ferryman. If there were no ferryman they could not meet each other. Furthermore, if there were heavy rain, the ferryman could not sail the boat. Thus their tryst was

Shenandoah

Sung by Jimmy Rodgers
Arr. by Elie Siegmeister

Slowly, sustained

Oh, Shen-an-doah. I long to hear you, A-

way, my rol-ling riv-er. Oh, Shen-an-doah, I_can't get near you. A-way, a-

way, I'm bound a-way 'Cross the wide Mis-sour-i

impossible. The boy wanted to meet when the camellia flower came out. The girl hesitated to meet him because of other people's eyes. Thus, she suggested that he wait until the camellia flower bloomed and the color of camellia got dark.

The boy waited from early fall on watching the color of the camellia flower. At last the day came. However, unfortunately it began to rain. It poured. In the early morning he rushed to the spot where the ferryboat was at anchor. The river was full with the water due to heavy rain. He could not cross over the Auraji River by boat even when he begged the ferryman to help. The ferryman just looked high up in the sky.

Oh, ferryman of Auraji River

Take me over the river
Blossom of oldongbak (camellia)
In Ssarigol are falling down
Arirang, Arirang, Arariyo
Pass me over the Arirang Hill

Between two folksong, Arirang and Shenandoah there are many similar points :

① The tune of Arirang and Shenandoah is very alike: peaceful, lonely and sad. Both folksong smooth over those feelings and mood with subtle touch.

② We don't know the origin of Arirang exactly; neither do we know the origin of Shenandoah.

③ For both folksong, the composer and the lyricist remain unidentified.

④ The cradle of Arirang is the Auraji River in Jeongseon. Shenandoah was originated around the Missouri River in Mississippi.

⑤ Arirang was regarded as a love song between a man and a woman. Shenandoah is also classified as a love song.

The items listed above present my personal view. The Auraji and the Missouri Rivers will flow endlessly. Likewise, both folksong will be sung forever.

4. Unforgatable People Relating to the Song of Arirang

a. Court Music and Tanabe Hisao

From 1921 to 1926, Tanabe Hisao investigated Joseon Dynasty's Court Music with Tada Tadasuke. They were interested in oriental music. Especially, Tanabe Hisao studied how the music of Joseon, Baekje, Silla and Goguryeo was conveyed to Japan and how the music developed in Japan. Through the studies, he figured out that Court Music of Japan, which is beloved worldwide originally, came from Joseon.

His book *Study of the Music of Ancient Japan*, tell us that "today, the Court Music of Japan is a world famous music. The Court Music was created and improved by migrants from Baekje, Silla and Goguryeo. It is played even in these days. In other words, the famous court music of Japan was created by Joseon people."

Not only did he contribute to the study of Joseon's music, but also he introduced Arirang into Japan. Since he was an instructor in the music school at the Royal Palace of Japan in 1921, he knew about Joseon music. Then, the GGJ had a plan to dissolve the Royal Court Music Orchestra of Joseon. Because of financial difficulties, the GGJ could not manage them. So the government suggested that either the National Zoo or the Royal Court Music Orchestra should be dissolved. At last, GGJ decided to dismiss the Royal Court Music Orchestra. Tanabe did not agree and opposed the idea to dissolve the Royal Court Music Orchestra.

According to him, "we can buy animals from foreign countries whenever we would like to. However, music and dance are very difficult to recover once they're destructed. It would go out of existence in the world. I believe that the Court Music of Joseon is great. So I will go to Joseon and prove the necessity of the preservation. I will help to preserve the Court Music."

On April 1, 1921, he arrived in Joseon. On his arrival, he studied and investigated the Royal Court Music of Joseon Dynasty closely. And he visited the women entertainers' training school in Pyongyang. He observed films and dancing for two weeks.

After returning to Japan, he decided to preserve the court music. Thanks to his effort, the ancient music of Joseon was spared. Moreover, he was introduced to Arirang. In an article, *Folksong and Politics of Joseon*, he pointed out the relationship between music and politics. He examined the people living at subsistence level because of under-education and bad climate. He mentioned that even though they suffered from poverty, they sang a beautiful and elegiac song, the song of Arirang. He made a chronological table of the Court Music. According to the table, Arirang became famous since the end of 1800s.

Tanabe made a motion picture regarding the Royal Court Music of Joseon Dynasty. The dancers and performers in the motion picture belonged to the GGJ. The film was played in Seoul, and was favorably commented on. They made a copy of the film. Later, the copy was sent to Tanabe in Tokyo while the original was kept with the Joseon royal family. The film was shown in schools, and conferences in Japan. Tanabe kept the film in his house. However, one day, Korean Independence activists visited him and asked to borrow the film. They promised to return it after they made a copy. Although he trusted them and gave it, the film had never got back to him. In addition, the original film which was in the Joseon royal family's house was presumed to be lost. There is a rumor that the film is in Japan.

b. Professor Choi Bok-hyun and the Song of Arirang

In my days as a student, I had the fortune of meeting one of the most influential Professors in Korea, Professor Choi Bok-hyun teacher at his alma mater, Choongang High School, located in Gye-dong, Seoul.

After his appointment as a teacher, it seems that he was not happy about his job. He was forced to give lectures justifying the Japanese occupation of Korea, which caused him great consternation. Historically, Choongang High School was strictly censored, and students were strictly steered away from having anti-Japanese sentiments. Because of this, his Geography class was never taught according go the syllabus. He always talked about the injustice of the Japanese occupation of Korea, which was an unlawful act of intrusion. The Koreans would have to stand up for themselves and claim their independence eventually, he said.

Sometimes he would ask leading questions. He asked the students if anyone knew how many railway stations we had from Seoul to Daejeon and Daejoen to Busan. The student bodies were smart enough to catch what their teacher's intentions were. They began to organize the anti-Japanese club. The membership of the club increased little by little, and it was soon over a dozen or so.

They met every weekend at the campus after school, or at the outskirts, in order to establish the club's goals at first. However, unfortunately, police officers raided their meeting place one day and arrested them all. They were placed under investigation at Jongno Police Station.

Choi appeared himself in front of the police officers, then told them that "all their mistakes were caused by me. Please release them all. Instead, I will take their all responsibility. Please arrest me." All the students were released and he was arrested in their place. His case was brought to the court and he received a verdict of guilty. He was imprisoned at Hamheung Prison in North Korea.

I thought he had a hard time during his imprisonment. Because he was classified as a political offender, he must have been treated particularly badly, even in addition to the extremely cold weather. Furthermore, he had few or no chances to meet his family because of the immense distance between Seoul in the South and Hamheung in the North.

His heart was full of bitterness and rebelliousness. To comfort his wounded heart each day, he sang of Arirang.

Fortunately, Japan lost the war and he was soon released. After he returned home, he spent some time at his home town, and later, he was appointed as a faculty member at the College of Education, Seoul National University.

I was one of his students during my undergraduate and graduate school days, and he was also my academic advisor. I spent much time under his guidance until I left for my studies in the US. I can say that I was much influenced by him. After I obtained my Ph.D degree, I returned to Korea, but by then, he was already on his sick bed due to an illness.

In fall 2011, a group of his former students, now all Professors, visited his grave located in Yangju, Gyeonggi-do Province. After a brief memorial ceremony, we spent time sharing stories of our old school days. By that time, Professor Hyong Kie-joo said that in the 1960s, they had a field work around the Gangnam area. After lunchtime, they held a sideshow time with students and faculty members.

That sideshow went on, and finally, it was Professor Choi's

turn, but he hesitated to sing, or to do anything at all. However, all the members clapped their hands, expressing their desire to hear his song. All of them were eager to listen to his song. All the students clapped their hands on and on. Then, finally, Professor Choi stood up and began to sing the song of Arirang. All of them were so pleased to hear his song of Arirang.

Professor Choi Bok-hyun

After this story, all of my friends began to sing the song of Arirang in front of his grave.

Arirang Arirang Arariyo
Arirang Gogaero Neomeoganda
Nareul Beorigo Gasineunnimeun
Simnido Motgaseo Balbyeongnanda

The student group mentioned above all became successful after they finished their studies. Together, they raised funds for a scholarship, which was titled with their teachers name- "Choi Bok-hyun Scholarship."

c. Han Yu-han "Korean opera Arirang"

At the age of nine, Han Yu-han moved to Beijing with his father, Han Heung-gyo. He received his bachelor's degree in Beijing, and participated in the anti-Japanese movements after the 1931 Manchurian Incident. After being active in the anti-Japanese movement in Shandong, he moved to Xi'an and joined the Chinese Military Authority Training Group and the Liberation Army.

In 1941, he formed the Arirang Band to lift the morale of the Liberation Army troops. He conducted opera Arirang related to love between man and woman, and anti-Japanese story.

On May 15, 1940 at Xi'an. Also he composed "Amnokgang March."

Composer Han Yu-han

"Amnokgang March" is one of the few independence anthems clearly attributed to the creators. This song, enjoyed by the Liberation Army soldiers, was written by Park Young-man and composed by Han Yu-han. The lyrics are as follows.

We are the Liberation Army, warriors to reclaim our nation

Let us march, let us march, crossing the Amnokgang and over the Baekdusan

We are the Independence Army, repelling the diabolic enemy, our foe

Let us march, let us march, crossing the Amnokgang and over the Baekdusan

The purity of our motherland has been changed into hell

Everyone is suffering from pain and wandering

Our countrymen are waiting

Let us return to our homes

There we see the brother crying under a lantern

There we see the flower trampled by the enemy

Our countrymen are waiting

Let us return to our motherland

We are the Liberation Army, warriors to reclaim our nation

Let us march, let us march, crossing the Amnokgang and over the Baekdusan

This song was presented in Korea for the first time on April 13, 1982, at the Sejong Center for the Performing Arts, at the 63rd Anniversary of the Provisional Government of the Republic of Korea, directed by Han Yu-han himself.

Song of Arirang in
the Hymn and Lullaby

Korean Peninsular viewed from the Sangjeongbawi Rock(Jeongseon)

9

Chapter

1. Arirang in the Hymnal of the United Presbyterian Church

When Christians go to church on Sundays, they sing many different hymns during the service. Since starting on this book, I discovered that Arirang has been included in the hymnal (364, 1990 version) that is used in the United Presbyterian Church in the US The title is *Christ, You are the Fullness* with subscript of *Tune: Arirang*.

I raised a question regarding this matter. How could the Korean folksong have been included in the hymnal for the United Presbyterian Church in the US? I started collecting information from the library and the Internet.

I did get some insights on this matter after I contacted Professor Bert Polman. He was working on the rearrangement of a hymnal in the Christian Reformed Church. He sent his reply shown below after we talked about Arirang as one of hymns in his edition.

I was a member of the editorial committee that produced the PSALTER HYMNAL for the Christian Reformed Church in

1987. It was our intention to include representative texts and/or tunes from beyond Europe and North America, and thus that hymnal included some hymns from Africa, Latin America and Asia. The tune "Arirang" was the only tune that our Korean consultants mentioned. At the same time, we were looking for some Scripture paraphrase text (based on the letter to the Colossians), with the intention that it be sung to the (slightly altered) version of the tune "Arirang."

The following is what I wrote about this tune in the *PSALTER HYMNAL HANDBOOK* (1998, page 364) : The tune ARIRANG is named after a Korean folksong that has long been a favorite in Korea and became known by many American soldiers during the Korean War (1950-1953). The song was probably composed around 1865, when laborers were conscripted from all over Korea to rebuild the Gyeongbokgung Palace in Seoul. These workers brought their regional folksong with them; this one presumably came from the legendary Arirang Mountains, which in Korean culture symbolize the sometimes bitter separation of loved ones. Arirang is a lament with romantic connotations; the original text can be translated :

As the stars, my tears are countless
As they ceaselessly flow!
You, so faithless, are leaving me alone and pale.
May your feet pain you at the end of the trail!
Arirang is a fascinating tune featuring repeats of complete

Christ, You Are the Fullness

Arirang Irregular

Vers. Bert Polman, 1986

Korean melody
Harm. Dale Grotenhuis, 1986

1. Christ, You are the full - ness of God, first - born of ev - ery-thing.
2. Since we have been raised with You, Lord, help keep our hearts and minds
3. Help us live in peace as true mem-bers of Your bod - y.

For by You all things were made; You hold them up.
Pure and set on things that build Your rule o'er all the earth.
Let Your word dwell rich - ly in us as we teach and sing.

The musical score of Hymn # 364

phrases and small motifs. Polman changed one of the original cadence patterns to make four clear phrases for this song, which is intended for unison singing. The 1986 keyboard harmonization by Dale Grotenhuis(another member of the Psalter Hymnal Committee) features a drone in the bass, a device common in much Asian music. Because of the irregular number of syllables in each stanza, have a soloist or choir introduce it to the congregation.

Polman is a Professor of music at Calvin College, Grand Rapids, Michigan and a Senior Research Fellow for the Calvin Institute of Christian Worship. He served on the Revision Committee the 1987 edition of the Psalter Hymnal.

The aforementioned information identifies clearly the reason why Arirang has been included in the hymnal of the United Presbyterian Church. The church believed that Arirang was worthy of being Joseon as a tune for a hymn because it had an attractive and appealing melody for worshiping God. The following section will show the detailed information of Arirang(Hymn 346). The English verse of Hymn 346 is a versification of Colossian 1:15-18("Who is the image of the invisible God, the firstborn of every creature…"). The whole verse is follows:

Christ, you are the fullness of God, first born of everything. For by you all things were made; you hold them up.

You are head of the church, which is your body.
First born from the dead, you in all things are supreme!

Since we have been raised with You, Lord, help keep our hearts and minds.
Pure and set on things that build your rule over all the earth.
All our life is now hidden with you in God.
When you come again we will share your glory.

Help us live in peace as true members of your body.
Let your word dwell richly in us as we teach and sing.
Thanks and praise be to God through you, Lord Jesus.
In whatever we do let your name receive the praise!

The popular folk-tune of Arirang resonates with the audience by combining with solemn words and beautiful harmonies that produce a delightful mood. It prepares the people to come closer to God and make confession to Him.

2. An Adopted Child and A Hymn

Initially, I expected that the Korean Consultant for a hymn committee had a particular reason to recommend the song of Arirang as a tune of a hymn. However, I found interesting information from Emily Brink, one of colleagues of Polman. I received an e-mail from Brink who is an editor (emeritus), reformed Worship at the Calvin Institute of Christian Worship.

In the early 1980s, when working on our revision of the Psalter Hymnal, the Revision Committee appointed four "Ethnic Consultants"(Asian, African American, Native American, and Hispanic); we invited them for consultations, and then received lists of song recommendations from three of those consultants-who in turn had gathered groups of people to assist them in making recommendations. But our Asian consultant, a Korean from California who was recommended by one of our CRC agencies, never responded or participated in that process. ARIRANG was recommended by Rev. David Koll, a pastor in Southern California who had adopted a

Korean child and pleaded with the Revision Committee to include at least one Korean song for the sake of the many Korean children who had been adopted, as well as entire Korean congregations coming to the US and joining the CRC. I believe he was the one who first recommended that this tune at least would be known and recognized. In checking with a few Korean pastors, we got mixed reactions to using this tune as the basis for a new Christian and biblical text. But some pastors were positive and said that North Americans certainly would not have problems of association with the Korean folksong. Now that more Koreans are part of the Christian Reformed Church, perhaps the association is more of a problem. Some of our English hymn tunes similarly have folksong roots, whose original texts have since faded from use.

In our new collection of songs, we included the Korean song "O So So"(#209 in Sing! A New Creation); as we learn of more songs from Korea directly composed as songs for worship, we will be glad to include them in future publications.

According to Brink, the professional consultant had not even responded, and a Pastor (David Koll) who adopted Korean children recommended the song of Arirang. Here is an e-mail Rev. David Koll sent to me :

Yes, Emily Brink told me of your note contacting her. My wife and I have two children, both adopted from Korea, both as infants, one in 1984 and one in 1987.(Yes, both are now in college!) We were living in eastern Michigan at the time, 1 hour north of Detroit in the community of Flushing, Michigan. For our adoption we worked with an agency called Bethany Christian Services(now a very large adoption agency, in many states). They had a partnership with the Holt Agency in Korea, and the Korean adoption program was very active - the culture of Korea made Korean adoption there very difficult, and there were many children being born to unwed mothers ··· In my recollection, 300-600 children per year were being adopted from Korea into Michigan-so there were many little Korean babies in our area of Michigan. We formed an "adoptive parents" club, and I was instrumental in starting a "summer camp" for the kids to learn Korean Culture. We received wonderful help from a local Korean Presbyterian Church, and my church also allowed the facility to be used for these purposes. So, in the mid 1980s as our denomination, the CRC, was preparing a new hymn book, and as the "value" of having "international songs" was one value offered, and as I knew that in the CRC there were a numbers of Korean congregations, I looked at the early drafts of the hymn book for a Korean song-and found none. I talked to Emily Brink (who I knew personally), and she gave me the same explanation she gave to you. So, not knowing much Korean music, I suggested that we use the Arirang tune, since that tune was used at about every Korean cultural gathering I had attended.

Emily took the tune to her committee, and they put the
Bible words to the tune, and the song ended up being selected.
Hope that fills in the detail you desire. Blessings to you,

David Koll

According to Pastor David Koll, a number of children are adopted from Korea every year. During the Korean War, many kids lost their parents and homes. The kids were sent to different countries to find a new family and home. As they grew up, they had a hard time finding their identity. Some of them tried to forget their biological family; some of them tried to find themselves and to clarify the identity. In the case of those who tried to find their roots, they met the biological parents and family and learned Korean. I can sympathize with them thinking of my early days in the US. As I have lived in US for about 40 years, singing Arirang in a Korean party is neither unfashionable nor awkward to me. I usually sing Arirang whenever I miss my parents and siblings of my home country.

As we see in the letter from Pastor David Koll, many adopted kids, students studying abroad, and immigrants are connected with Korea by Arirang. Since they live in foreign countries, they may miss Korea. Arirang has always been there for them. The love for the country and their parents could have made Arirang one of hymns. Wherever Koreans go, many Koreans sing Arirang. Arirang is spreading to the world with Koreans. The song becomes a universal song.

3. Arirang of as a Cradle Song and Classical Music

No record exists about the composer or lyricist writer of Arirang. The song of Arirang has only been sung mouth to mouth, over and over, so the song has become a part of Korean life. People sing Arirang to get rid of suffering or to cheer up. Arirang has been also included in a classical music CD *Cantate Domino*.

Most Koreans recognize and regard Arirang as folksong, but not as classical music. So, how can a Korean folksong be arranged as a lullaby and be included in the classical music? This unusual story is associated with the famous conductor, Sir Harold Malcolm Watts Sargent(April 29, 1895-October 3, 1967).

He was an English organist and composer widely known as a leading conductor of choral works in Britain. The musical ensembles with which he was involved were the Ballets Russes, the Royal Choral Society, the D'Oyly Carte Opera Company, and the London Philharmonic, Halle, Liverpool Philharmonic, BBC Symphony and Royal Philharmonic orchestras.

We cannot find any record about when he arranged the Arirang to a lullaby or why he did it. However, as I learned of his career and life through his biography, I came to know that he was interested in foreign music.

He visited many foreign countries. He had been to South America twice. In 1950, he conducted in Buenos Aires, Montevideo, Rio de Janeiro and Santiago. In the 1960s, Sargent visited Russia, US, Canada, Turkey, Israel, India, Northeast Asia and Australia. Northeast Asia refers to Korea, China, Japan and Mongolia. He could have visited Korea or heard Arirang. As he arranged the song, Arirang also received much recognition as a classical music.

LULLABY

A mother nurses her sick child
(Korean Folk Song)

Words and music
arranged by
MALCOLM SARGENT

* To-fa, pronounced 'Toh-fah' = 'Sleep'. The bass should be legato and continuous in sound.

★★ *Each verse to be repeated.* The tenors do *not* sing the first time, but sing in the repeat of each verse.

Similarity to Arirang

The East Sea sited on the eastern part of Korean Peninsula

10
Chapter

1. Arirang

The intellectual class in Korea continuously ignored the song of Arirang. They thought Arirang belonged to the lower class. Since 1980, however, Arirang has become widely accepted as the foremost folksong of Korea. Arirang was sung by the people whenever they were sad, joyful, or bitter. In a sense, Arirang represents the history of the Korea itself. Whenever we listen to Arirang, it touches our hearts because it is a reflection of genuine Korean sentiment.

Language, custom, ideology, belief and social life were all mixed in Arirang to create a folksong. Arirang represents the soul of Koreans and it is a Korean people's eternal hometown and motherland.

During the Japanese occupation Arirang was always with them. It was the symbol of resistance, solidarity and forgiveness. Arirang has some similarities to other folksong like Yankee Doodle, Samba, Chanson and Tango soon.

First, the folksongs were likely to be underestimated or ignored. But lower class people loved them and kept them.

Second, although folksongs described popular sorrow, pain, and life, they seldom describe hope. People combat their agony by singing the songs.

Third, Tango, Chanson and Arirang were treated badly but they have survived to date. Among them Chanson has the longest history. Despite such a hard time, it has survived 20 centuries. Because of this, the songs always touch on our hearts. Fourth, Yankee Doodle Samba, Tango, Chanson, Jazz, and Arirang are simple and easy. Anyone can learn and memorize them with ease.

Even if it might be well nigh imposible to put them all in the same category, they do have some things in common: about their creation and the social backgrounds of the people who created them.

2. Yankee Doodle

There is a history between Arirang and Yankee Doodle. The origin of Yankee Doodle has not been found like Arirang. The tune Yankee Doodle encountered the song of Arirang in Korea.

On May 22, 1882, Korea and the US signed a treaty for diplomatic relations. Historically, this Korean-US diplomatic agreement was the first treaty Korea ever made with a western country. After this agreement, the Korean government was supposed to be open to a foreign country which wanted to have a relationship with Korea.

Commander Robert Shufeldt was the representative of the US and Kim Hong-jip represented Korea. Prior to the offical signing, Americans hoisted their national flag, the Stars and the Stripes, and were going to play their National Anthem. Korea also raised a flag on which a tiger was drawn as its national flag. However, Korea did not have official National Anthem. So Commander Shufeldt took the situation into consideration, the Marine band of America played Yankee

Yankee Doodle

American Folk Song
Arr. by Joseph Lee

Con spirito

Father and I went down to camp, A long with Captain Good -
And there we see a thou-sand men, As rich as Squire ___

Good - ing And there we saw the men and boys As thick as ha - sty
Da - vid; And what they wast-ed ev - ry day, I wish it could-be

pud - ding. Yan - kee Doo-dle keep it up Yan - kee Doo-dle
sav - ed. Yan - kee Doo-dle keep it up Yan - kee Doo-dle

dan - dy, Mind the mu-sic and the step,And with the girls be han - dy.
dan - dy, Mind the mu-sic and the step,And with the girls be han - dy.

Doodle instead of the National Anthem of America and they performed the song of Arirang for Korea. This historical fact proved that the song of Arirang was regarded as National Anthem.

"Yankee Doodle" is a well-known British song of which origin dates back to the Seven Year's War. It has been widely adopted in the US and is often sung patriotically today. It is the state anthem of Connecticut.

A part of the a full version of the song is quoted as follows:

Yankee Doodle went to town
A riding on a pony,
Stuck a feather in his cap
And called it Macaroni!

Chorus :
Yankee Doodle Keep it up,
Yankee Doodle dandy,
Mind the music and the step
And with the girls be handy.

3. Samba

Samba Show (Carnival) is held at the beginning of February in Rio de Janeiro, Brazil. A large number of people visit Rio de Janeiro during the Carnival to see the Samba Show. During the Carnival, Rio de Janeiro as well as the whole of Brazil, turns into a melting pot of peoples with the passion of Samba.

There are a few different views. Regarding the origin of Samba First, it is assumed that it was created by native Africans. Samba music has a 2/4 beat rhythm. It is fast dance music. Second, people say that Samba music was created when the slaves from Africa tried to show their ability to their masters. The third and the most persuasive view is that people coming from Portugal to Brazil let their African slaves play their traditional percussion instruments and dance to celebrate Lent. Thus the Samba was born.

In the early 1930s, Samba was performed on small scale in several villages. Afterwards, they set up Samba schools and the schools gave parade shows. Since then, it has developed

Samba Festival in Rio de Janeiro, Brazil

into a large scale show as known today. The show has grown so rapidly and it is the biggest festival in the world.

Samba schools are for the Samba Show. Anyone who wants to enter Samba schools may be accepted. Then they spend a

year engaged in the preparation for the Carnival Samba Show. The hightlight of the Rio de Janeiro Carnival is definitely the Samba parade. The dancers participate in the parade and big bands play music in the street.

Samba Show is one of the biggest events in the world. Its birth goes back to the 19th century. This Samba Show is a unique festival. They adopted the drum rhythm and dance.

Brazil has developed this unique festival overcoming cultural and racial boundaries. Big bands play music while the dancers dance with strength and energy on big carriage carts. The streets of Rio de Janeiro turned into a melting pot.

Today Samba Show is managed by the tourism office of the Brazilian government. About 4,000 to 5,000 people make up a group and then participate in the show as a team. Among them there are special groups called A-class teams (total of 14 teams). To be selected as an A-class team, countless teams compete in front of

70,000 spectators at the central railway station (Sambadromo).

In order to impress the audience within one hour and 20 minutes, the participants do their best. Rio de Janeiro prepares Samba Show thoroughly. To be admitted in the main place of the Samba Show spectators have to pay US$ 20.00-US$ 300.00. When the demand is high, the tickets are sold on the black market.

It frequently rains during this time of the year. The temperature goes up to 30°C, sometimes reaching 40°C. Despite the humidity and temperature, they do their best to get a high score. The spectators are filled with admiration. After the judges decide on the champion at the end of the Samba Week, the champion parades again. They are awarded US$ 2,000,000.

Also, if someone fails to get the ticket for the A-class Samba Show in Rio de Janeiro, it is advisable to see B or C class show.

I should also point out that there is little discrimination against minor ethnic or racial groups. Over 80 ethnic groups live in harmony in Brazil. There is no room to practice segregation. You can hardly feel the tension of racial discrimination. If someone causes a problem with reference to discrimination, the Brazilian government will immediately send him or her to a prison for a 5-year imprisonment. Brazil occupies almost half of all South America. Without any racial discord, the people live together peacefully. They are doing a wonderful job passing on its beautiful nature to the next generation.

While observing the Samba Show in Brazil, I was thinking of Arirang Festival in Korea. We can add more entertaining elements to Arirang Festival, such as a fashion show, a ceramic ware show, Samullori(Korean folk music accompanied by the percussion) and a Gugak(Korean traditional music) concert. If we adopt something unique for Arirang Festival, the festival will attract more people year by year like the Samba Carnival. I hope someday Arirang Festival can be like three other great festivals:

① The Samba Show, February in Rio de Janeiro
② The Germany Beer Festival, October
③ The Japanese Snow Festival

The winter Arirang Festival is held annually making use of all existing Arirang in Korea. I think that there is a possibility for Arirang Festival to grow like the Lorelei Festival of Germany or the Yodle Festival of Switzerland.

Arirang is one of the most charming folksongs. It has become a world famous song thanks to the 1986 Asian Games, the 1988 Olympic Summer Games, and the 2002 FIFA World Cup Korea/Japan. Anyone who visited Korea during these events must have learned the song of Arirang.

Sometime ago, I read the *New York Times* reporting about kimchi's excellence as the food of Korea. Today kimchi is known to the world as well as the song of Arirang. In this regard it should be a good idea to provide various types of food during Arirang Festival. Food is indispensable to festivals. People are usually interested in cuisine of other countries. Without tasting Korean food they cannot fully understand Korean culture.

In this regard I suggest they sell delicious Korean traditional food sometimes combined with western food at Arirang Festival. If the tourists are given a chance to sample the food in person, it will be an unforgettable experience. There could be many ways to make the Arirang Festival more colorful.

4. Tango

Argentina in Latin America is the birthplace of Tango, Tango was born in Barrio Boca, a small port located about 5km away from Buenos Aires. This Tango melody was similar to that of the Samba in Brazil and that of Jazz in the US They are both delicate and sentimental.

Tango is accompanied by dance and cheerful music, in a 2/4 rhythm. The fundamental rhythm was originated from African dance which the black slaves took to Cuba and Haiti. There's also the influence of European traditional music in Tango. Tango prospered especially in Argentina. Regarding why Tango was created in Argentina, there are two stories. One explains that sailors introduced Cuban music to Argentina in the early 19th century. The Cuban music was mixed with popular songs of that time, and finally Tango was born in Argentina.

The Argentine Tango has sadness and strong feelings in it and also expresses strong passion. Tango is unique because it has both long and short scales in the same song. In 1910, it was introduced to Europe (such as Paris or London), where it was welcome. Being popular in Europe, Tango became one of the world's beloved musical types.

Barrio Boca is famous as the birthplace of Tango and has been inhabited by poor people. They were immigrants from Italy or sailors landing from their rough voyage. They were poor, hopeless, and depressed. They hung around cheap bars. Life was tough. They had no dream or future. They just chatted and drank. Because of this, Tango has s sorrowful mood. Even thought Tango gradually became popular and was accepted by high society, it retained the original color.

In Argentina, whenever and wherever music is played, it will accompany dance. In the evening, they may enjoy Tango, food and drink everywhere. Sailors and laborers step into a Tango bar to enjoy themselves. They talk about love and dreams. Sometimes in Tango they find a vent to their unattainable love and dreams.

In Barrio Boca, there were sailors and laborers who missed their homes, families and loved ones. They danced to express all the feelings. A man and a woman danced to burn themselves out with passion. Even though Europeans felt somewhat uncomfortable with Tango, the passion of Tango eventually fascinated Europeans.

Tango is the music of Argentina without question. Recently, it is difficult to see a Tango performance even in Buenos Aires.

First class theaters and restaurants don't present Tango performances. One has to head to taverns. Originally Tango was born in rugged taverns. People can feel the real sorrow and passion of Tango in such taverns. Whenever I listen to Tango or other folksongs, I feel the greatness of grass-roots songs. There is their happiness, sorrow, joy and pleasure in Tango.

The British physicist John Tyndall(1820-1893) made the following statement : "a human mind is similar to the instrument which has a regular scale. However, beyond the both ends of musical scales, there are endless sounds in it. Tango was created within this endless zone of musical scale. People stuck in the regular musical scale cannot create music like Tango. Tango was created clearly by the people who are standing beyond the musical scale. They are sailors, the unemployed, gang members, the heartbroken and vagabonds. But in 1918, Tango, created by the poor, was introduced to Europeans. Then Tango became popular. Tango came back to Argentina in 50 years. Originally Tango was born among the poor people. In the tone, there are sadness and some feeling leading to sadness. Tango reflects the tough life in Latin America by the tone. Tango is definitely the representative music in Argentina.

5. Chanson

Chanson was conveyed mouth to mouth at in early century. In French, Chanson means a song. The origin of Chanson will be traced to the common people.

During the 16th century, a few lyrical poets composed Chansons. J. J. Rousseau (1712-1778) stated in his work *Musical Dictionary* (1760) that Chanson is short lyrical words. People sang Chanson when they felt comfortable.

According to Rousseau, the French sang Chanson everywhere. Whenever they were tired or engaged in hard work they sang Chanson. He categorized Chanson as follows :

① Love song
② Wine song
③ Satirical song

Chanson was ignored for a long time as other types of folksong were. Chanson is easy to listen to. We can listen to Chanson with ease as it absorbs us like the sponge absorbs water quickly. It provides fresh flavor. In the late 20th century famous musicians who loved Chanson composed many Chansons to promote the position of Chanson.

Chanson is, and will be the song of common people. Therefore, Chanson should be simple and easy to memorize. The words should be plain and should touch the hearts of people as well. Chanson has a sorrowful sound. Chanson represents the mind and feelings of the singer.

6. Jazz

Let me briefly examine the trend of international music. Africa was one of the most prominent centers of music in the 20th century thanks to the opulence of African music. Black people in Africa were taken to the US and to the West Indies to work on the plantation farms as slaves. They spent all their time on the farms enduring discrimination. During this period, they sang in order to console themselves.

Gradually their songs were mixed with the songs of the US. Thus, colored people produced so-called Jazz in the US and it spread all over the world. Jazz is a remarkable genre. Eventually African music has shaped the music of the 20th century. The creativeness and cultural exchanges are distinctive features of the 20th century. It was a turning point in modern music. As to Jazz, many countries in Latin America played an important role. The influence of Indio and colored people in the history of music should not be underestimated.

7. Danso of Korea and Quena of Latin America

We visited Peru and enjoyed a local song played by a Peruvian traditional instrument called "Quena."

Quena is a kind of flute. The music touched on my heart because its sound was very similar to that of the danso, a Korean traditional flute.

Koizumi Humio, a Japanese musician, once asked "How does the danso of Korea resemble Quena of Latin America?" and he conjectured on the cultural exchange between Korea and South America in the ancient times. Geographically, there is a sensible theory between Quena and the Andean area.

About 15,000 years ago, ancestors of native Americans ventured on a great human migration along the west coast of North America from Mongolia through the Bering Strait to North America. On their arrival, they spread out to all areas of South America. Especially, I am interested in the feature of music played by Quena. Quena has a unique tone. Its sound makes the audience sad. Under the Spanish colonization, playing Quena was banned. The Spanish were worried that

Danso   Quena

Quena could agitate conflict among the native people.

Quena is thought to be handed down from Atlantis. Today, Quena is made of wood, bamboo, PVC, or copper. In the early days, it was made from human bones, bones of one's loved ones. The structure is simple. It has finger holes and both ends are open. It can play various tunes depending on the player. Some say that every Quena has its own unique sound.

It has a delicate and subtle sound. Jang Deok-su says the Quena has a very sorrowful sound. That might be because the players and the audience of Quena music have pity for their ancestors who were destroyed by the Spanish colonialists. Or they might be missing their loved ones whose bone was made into Quena. The sound of Quena is sad. Quena looks like and sounds like the danso of Korean.

I wanted to study more about the similarity between them. That's why I brought the Quena with me from Peru. Deprived of everything during the Japanese occupation, Koreans had to leave their home and land. They sang Arirang in China, Japan and Russia. They missed their motherland while singing Arirang. Inevitably the song was sad. I think the song of Arirang and the Quena have similar tunes because Korea and Peru have similar historical backgrounds.

Takahashi Tohoru once mentioned about Arirang of North Korea. He wrote in his book *Folksong of North Korea* that the Arirang of North Korea sounded sadder than that of South Korea. He thought that the political factors in Korea were the cause of the sadness. It was difficult for people from the northern regions to become government officials. They expressed their grief and sadness by playing the danso and singing the song of Arirang under the moonlight in the ruins of ancient palaces. Arirang that shepherd boys sang returning home in the twilight ferryman sang on the boat floating on the Dumangang(Tumen) River sounded even lonelier.

Possibility of the Globalization of Arirang

A sea of clouds of Mt. Hambaeksan(Jeongseon)

11

Chapter

1. World Musicians who loved Arirang

The song of Arirang has recived a great attention around the world. One famous German Jazz group "Saltacello" played and recorded Arirang in a Jazz version. Moreover, the Munich Chamber Orchestra carried out the Korean Project to stimulate the cultural exchange between South and North Korea. Five of the members of the Munich Chamber Orchestra formed 'Arirang Quintet' to perform Arirang. Arirang Quintet enhanced the understanding of Arirang and the friendship between Germany and Korea. Arirang has been played in western countries such as the US. John Barnes Chance was a composer who wrote "Variations on a Korean Folksong" to play in front of an American audience in 1967. He heard Arirang in the late 1950s in Korea.

Moreover, several famed musicians of the world produced a recording of Arirang. For example, a famous Jazz pianist and singer Nat King Cole recorded Arirang on a live show edition in 1973. Also, Paul Mauriat of France visited Korea to perform a music concert in December 1975. Then on the next visit, she produced a new song of Arirang she herself arranged. The new version of Arirang by Paul Mauriat is somewhat European. He also made an album containing the song of Arirang. The title of the album is "*Arirang Miracle*." She made Arirang an international song. The leader of Saltacello, Peter Schindler, appraised that Arirang had

Jazz pianist and singer Nat King Cole

incredible energy inside. He compared the song of Arirang with the music of Wolfgang Amadeus Mozart. As one more word of praise, George Winston, an American pianist said that "I always play Arirang whenever I tour in concert in America. I think this is the world's best folksong. It could be the blues and excessive emotion simultaneously.

In addition, many famous musicians performed and produced new versions of Arirang to fit on their music. This is how Arirang became known to the world.

Arirang was adopted into the hymn of the Presbyterian Church. For example, in the hymn book(1990) 364 sections Arirang is recorded under the title *Christ, You Are the Fullness*.

Also, a record entitled *Cantate Domino* in which 15 world famous hymns were included was published in Sweden. The 7th track is the song of Arirang under the name of "Lullaby. "

Pianist George Winston

It was introduced: Whatever dreadful tidewater rushes into our side, this mysterious tune puts us to sleep. We feel as if we are set inside the mother's bosom. Thus, we fall into sleep peacefully.

Sleep in my arms, the birds homeward fly.
Sleep in my arms, the cool evening fall round thee
Sleep in my arms, little baby's mother is here
Sleep in my arms, thou frail weary one
Sleep in my arms, for thy Lord, watch o'er thee
Sleep in my arms, the sweet savior will keep thee from harm

Arirang is thought of as a peaceful song and it is sung as a hymn. I would like to look into the history of Arirang in the context of the history of the world. Korea had been frequently invaded by neighboring countries. Koreans sang Arirang and overcame the hard time. The Korean War is another good example. The Korean people went through the harsh days with Arirang. That's why those who fought in the Korean War remember Korea along with Arirang.

During the Korean War, many United Nations forces

participated. This occasion gave the soldiers a chance to hear the song of Arirang. Thus, the song was diffused all over the world. During that time, in order to console the UN forces, many entertainers and musicians visited Korea. Marilyn Monroe, who was a famous actress, stayed in Busan for four days (February 18, 1954 Dong-a Ilbo). Including noted singer Marian Anderson and comedian Bob Hope, about 300 entertainers visited Korea. When they were on the stage, they always played the song of Arirang.

Another example is Oscar Pettiford(1922-1960), a famous Jazz pianist, who visited Korea in 1951. He listened to the song of Arirang then he arranged it into a Jazz tune. Later he recorded it and named it *Ah Dee Dong*. The record was released by Royal Roots Company under the title *Music of the Future*.

At the beginning of October 1951, Oscar Pettiford came to Okinawa, Japan to entertain American soldiers. On the way home he stopped at Incheon Korea. He heard the song of Arirang then. After he returned home, he arranged the song and published it in his album. Later in 1981 this production was named *Discovery* which was his best collection. He sold it in the US and Germany. Also, one of his friends, the pianist

Jazz pianist Oscar Pettiford

Charles Mingus recorded it.

This was the first Jazz version of Arirang. Thus, the song of Arirang was arranged by world-class musicians. Thanks to their works, Arirang became widely known to all over the world and to Korean people as well. In addition, these events led Korea to the world of pop music. In this way, Korea became one of major markets of pop songs. Especially, 16 UN forces returned home with the song of Arirang they learned in the Korean War. It was a kind of souvenir. Thus, the song of Arirang was diffused over the world.

Relating to the visits of American musicians and entertainers, I would like to talk about Marian Anderson: I had an opportunity to attend a commencement held at the University of Michigan Field Stadium whose capacity was over 100,000. The keynote speaker was Marian Anderson. She is not white. She is a colored woman. I was moved to see this scene. I thought the US is a wonderful country. In this country if anyone has an excellent talent, and ability, there is plenty of room for them.

Seeing her and listening to her keynote address gave me a tremendous impression. I still remember one phrase she said, "Work hard and pursue your goal." I have a vivid memory of her. She well demonstrated her ability to serve this country. I am sure she had a chance to listen to Arirang while she visited Korea. She must have sensed the sadness and sentiment of the song in conjunction with the Negro spirituals.

2. The Nobel Prize Winners' Encounter with Arirang

Several Nobel Prize winners have made remarks about the song of Arirang:

Pearl S. Buck, a Nobel Prize winner in Literature(1938) visited Korea in order to find about Korea's traditional family system for her novel. She visited a village in Andong, Gyeongsangbuk-do Province. It was early 1940.

When she arrived at a village near Andong it was the evening. Buck saw a farmer heading for home with a cart pulled by an ox and a jige(an A-frame carrier) on his back. He was singing the song of Arirang. Buck stopped and got out of the car. She carefully observed the farmer. The cart was empty; the A-frame on his back was loaded with an empty lunch box. Buck was touched by this farmer especially when she saw the farmer treat the ox as a member of his family. She thought Koreans were peace-loving and nature-oriented people.

In 1962, she wrote *The Living Reed* based upon the life of Kim's family in Andong. She described three generations of the family in the novel. On the cover she wrote down the song

Pearl S. Buck

of Arirang. Buck was introduced the song of Arirang in a rural area in South Korea.

Oe Kenzaburo, a Japanese writer and Nobel Prize winner in Literature(1994) had a child, Hikari who was suffering from autism. He could neither speak nor cry. He had no tear pipe. His life seemed to be completely shut out from the outside world. However, he was very sensitive toward sound and noise.

Oe gave a special lecture to Korean people. It was his first visit to Korea. He had an interview with journalists in Seoul. On this occation, he also touched on his son's story, "When I was about to leave home for Korea, my son played the song of Arirang in room. He knew that I was going to Korea. Instead of saying good-by, he played the song." Oe was introduced the song of Arirang through his son's piano playing.

Hikari is now a musician in Japan. He commented on the Arirang as follows, "Arirang is a song of the past, but Korean people are still singing it. It will be continiously sung in the future. Through Arirang not only the Japanese but also people all over the world can understand Korea. So it is a wonderful

Oe Kenzaburo

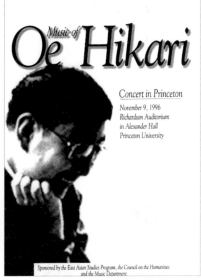

Music of **Oe Hikari**

Concert in Princeton
November 9, 1996
Richardson Auditorium
in Alexander Hall
Princeton University

Sponsored by the East Asian Studies Program, the Council on the Humanities
and the Music Department

his son, Oe Hikari

song to sing and talk about."

Kawabata Yasunari(1899-1972) Nobel Prize winner in Literature of 1968 had a relationship with the song of Arirang. He had no chance to visit Korea. However, by watching Arirang performance by Choe Seung-hui, a famous Korean womon dancer, Kawabata appreciated the song of Arirang. The Koreans are one of the most influencial groups on the globe. People listen to their appraisals or judgments. Several Nobel Prize winners have made remarks about the the song of Arirang.

3. The World Song Arirang

UNESCO gives an award to individuals or groups who study and preserve valuable oral folklores to pass down to the next generation. This award is named Arirang and UNESCO grants US$ 30,000 to the winner. Hereby, Arirang has become the symbol of the value of oral folklores. I believe the world has recognized the vitality and the historical power of Arirang, which is sung by overseas Koreans in 127 countries.

Now Arirang is a world song. Many have contributed to the diffusion of the song. For instance, at the end of the 19th century, exiles and refugees sang Arirang as a sad nostalgic song of their mother land. The missionaries recorded it as a sorrowful song on their travel journals. The veterans of the Korean War introduced the song to their homelands. In the 1980s, Arirang was reproduced by famous musicians. Indeed, the territory of Arirang is not confined to Korea; it has become a song of the world.

December 5, 2012, the Korean folksong *Arirang* has been registered on UNESCO's Representative List of Intangible

Cultural Heritage of Humanity.

UNESCO confirmed the registration submitted by the Caltural Heritage Administration of Korea at the 7th Intergovernmental Committee for the Safegurding of Intangible Cultural Heritage held in Paris, France, UNESCO day.

4. Kim Chan-sam and Arirang

Kim Chan-sam, former Professor of Kyung Hee University traveled all over the world carrying a backpack decorated with Taegeukgi(the national flag of Korea). He played a role as a nongovernmental diplomat. His friends wrote in the book *The Explorer and Geographer Kim Chan-sam*(2008) that he taught the song of Arirang in schools and villages whenever a chance was arose.

He and I were close friends since we were in Seoul National University. He sang and taught Arirang in such unfamiliar places as South America, Africa, and the Middle East. He was a pioneer of the diffusion of Arirang.

When he visited Togo in Africa, he was warmly welcomed by a school master who had met a Korean before in Stockholm, Sweden. The Korean he met was friendly and amicable. The school master, he gave a warm welcome to Kim Chan-sam. As usual he sang the song of Arirang. The song touched the hearts of many of the guests. The melody of Arirang was so humble and plain that the people of Togo were

Traveler, geographer and Professor Kim Chan-sam

able to learn the song of Arirang easily. As George Winston said, the song of Arirang is a universal song, beyond national and racial boundaries.

The Characteristics of Arirang

Ferry boat operated by chain floating on the Donggang River(Jeongseon)

12
Chapter

To study Arirang is comparable to discovering Korea. Arirang historically played a significant role in the life of Koreans. So, the song of Arirang is a living record of the history of Korean people and that of Korea as well.

Arirang has been closely tied with patriotic songs, martial songs, popular songs, and the songs of the times. Koreans have sung Arirang regardless of ideology and time. Today they sing the song of Arirang as a longing for the reunification of Korea.

1. Solidarity

In the past, Arirang played a significant role to bind Koreans together as one whether living in the homeland or overseas. Unfortunately, however, Korea is divided into two parts, South and North Korea. Arirang is still playing an important role to bind two the Koreas as one. For example, in some international events, South and North Korea appear as one country. When marching in the opening ceremony of the Olympic Games, they march together to the melody of Arirang. In the near future, Arirang will bring Korea together as one country.

Pete Seeger, the famous folksong writer, said, "Even though South and North Korea is are now fighting each other, someday they will unite as one country because they all sing Arirang. The song of Arirang might be a strong factor leading to the unification of Korea. They are one." This comment is persuasive. They will stand strong overcoming all the obstacles until they finally obtain the unification in the spirit of Arirang.

2. Resistance and Forgiveness

The second important factor is the spirit of resistance. Along this line, Koreans are closely united to fight. During the Japanese occupation of over 35 years, Korea was confronted with the imperialist Japanese government. Koreans obtained independence in 1945. Before 1945, however, large numbers of Korean nationalists and patriots were put in jail. Farmers were robbed of their land by Japanese authority and had to wander about in Manchuria, Siberia, or Hawaii.

Those people were in great pain, but never gave up their fighting with Japanese. Hardships were always overcome by the spirit of Arirang, which was the undying spirit of Koreans. Thus, Arirang goes with Koreans. Whenever they go, it is the mark of Koreans. The nature of Koreans is amicable and admirable. They are warm and gentle people unless they are treated unfairly. They know when to fight against injustice and when to forgive the act of hostility.

3. Long Continuity

Arirang has a long history. There is no other example in Korea like Arirang, which has been continiously sung by people for so many years. Yankee Doodle was born and became a popular folksong during the American Revolution. Yankee Doodle helped American people overcome the hardships and finally win their Independence.

The soldiers sang Yankee Doodle when they went to the war front to boost their morale. However, the song of Yankee Doodle has gradually disappeared.

Likewise, O Sole Mio in Italy, Lorelei in Germany, the Manyoshu in Japan, and Hyangga of the Silla in Korea are no longer sung or recited. They didn't survive a long time. Arirang, however, is still popular in Korea and in the world.

4. Easy to learn, Simple and Fascinating Melody

Arirang is simple and easy to learn. People can easily memorize the lyrics and the melody. They may sing the song to express joy, sorrow, happiness, love and hate. And there is no limitation to gender or age. The young and the old sing Arirang together. Arirang was created by common people.

Simply, Arirang exists in the heart of anyone who sings it. People say that a novel belongs to the reader and similarly, Arirang belongs to the singer. Koreans sing Arirang wherever they are. People of the world sing Arirang, too, as the melody is exceptionally fascinating, and touches the hearts of anyone regardless of race and culture.

Conclusion

A lady of Auraji and Pavilion(Jeongseon)

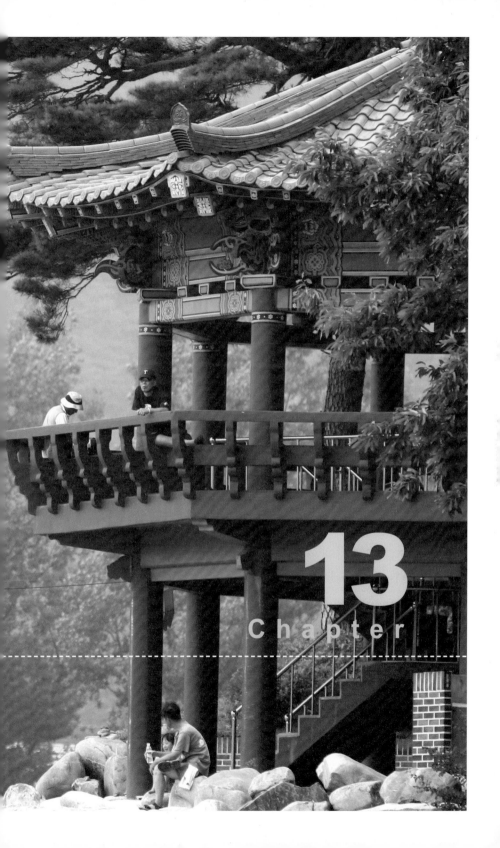

13

Chapter

1. My study on Arirang

Korean vocabularies have geographical nicknames for the country such as Hwaryeogangsan (beautiful mountains and rivers) or Hanbando (Korean Peninsula). There is a relatively new one, "Baekdudaegan", which has been popular since the 1980s.

Baekdudaegan is intended to represent the topography of Korea from South and North. Namely, it covers the provinces of Hamgyeong-do, Pyeongan-do, Gangwon-do, Chungcheong-do, Gyeongsang-do, and Jeolla-do. The new nickname of Korea appears to be the outcome of Korean's desire to express their life style itself instead of the land of Korea.

My research interest in geography has been population movement, land use planning, and geography of East Asia. I also taught remote sensing of the environment through my 50 years of professional career in Korea and abroad including America, Japan, Malaysia and China. One of my striking impressions is the apparent impact of Arirang on Korean culture and the life of Korean immigrants. In order to seek answers to the Arirang's role, I conducted a series of field trips for last five years to the places associated with Arirang in Korea. The places covered are Jindo in Jeollanam-do Province, Yeongcheon in Gyeongsangbuk-do Province and Jeongseon in Gangwon-do Province.

Through these field trips, I met many locals and scholars who provided valuable data and insight on Arirang's role in Korean life and culture. I have reached the conclusion that Arirang was more than a Korean folksong. Its impact on Korean culture and history has multiple dimensions. Therefore, Arirang deserves recognition as Korean cultural property. One particular inspiration for my Arirang research was to fulfill one of the important goals of human geography. Specifically, it is to delineate the value of ethnic culture and tradition.

Although I am gratified with what I have learned from my Arirang research, my current work on Arirang is far from complete. There are several places that I still wish to visit. These places include Hapgang-ri in Inje at the mouth of the Bukhangang River, Ulleungdo Island, and Jejudo Island. Also, I missed the famous Arirang festivals held in Daegu and Seongbuk in Seoul.

One of the reasons why I published this English version of Arirang is to provide additional information that I failed to include in my Korean version of Arirang. Before closing my Arirang project, I would like to list the specialists on Arirang who enlightened me on different phases of Arirang during my field trips.

They include Kim Yeon-gap, Ki Mi-yang, Park Min-Il, Park Byeong-hun, Jeong Mun-gyo, Kim Jin-dong and Kim Dae-jin, Yu Jae-man and summarize what I have learned from many scholars, their papers, field trips and discussions with Arirang specialists. I believe that they have provided valuable and diverse knowledge of Arirang. I have tried to present as many different aspects of Arirang as best I can.

2. Consilience Approach for Studying Arirang

Biologist Edward O. Wilson (1929-) introduced the word of "consilience" in 1998 to describe the synthesis of knowledge from different specialized fields of human study. Recently, columnists and Professor Lee O-young and Shin Yong-ha discussed the significance of consilience through their columns in Korean newspapers. Wilson's consilience may be a valuable tool to study Arirang because of the complexity of its history and impact on Koreans.

How did Arirang start? What did the word of Arirang originate from? What type of scientific method would be suitable for Arirang study? Why and how did Arirang reach so many people in the world far away from Korea? Why has Arirang become the folksong of Korea while there are many other Korean folksongs? What is the spirit of Arirang? And what should be the role of Arirang in Korean society today? Wilson's approach may be helpful to answer these questions related to Arirang study. Many studies have addressed the questions on Arirang, but the scope of Arirang discussion has been limited to Korean literature and folk music. In order to tackle the questions listed above, we have to establish the Arirang study as an independent discipline of study such as science of Arirang. We must be bold enough to broaden our horizons of Arirang research. We should not be content with the mere conservation of Arirang culture.

Also, there should be an academic institute and museum solely dedicated to Arirang so that researchers can get access to various types of Arirang information. One possible location for the museum would be Insa-dong in Seoul considering its easy access to tourists. Also, because it is the cradle of the song of Arirang imperishable history and because of the tradition and beautiful natural environment and the unspoiled and amicable people of Jeongseon, it's desirable to set up a National Arirang Research Institute in Jeongseon, Gangwon-do Province. Through these channels, Arirang's spirit and culture would spread throughout the world.

Arirang could serve as a cardinal hallmark of Korea. I believe Arirang is more appropriate as a symbol of Korea than any other alternatives such as Taekwondo, kimchi or tigers. All of these could represent embody Korea well, but Arirang is the most appealing due to its rich history and its tremendous impacts on Koreans. In addition, Arirang represents the Korean people's love of music. It is also easy for foreigners to learn as Arirang is easy to memorize and sing. These features help foreigners get acquainted with Korean culture.

3. Arirang Festivals and Common Theme

I was fortunate to visit and appreciate Yeongcheon Arirang Festival in 2005 and DMZ Arirang Festival in Cheorwon in 2006. I also reviewed Jeongseon Arirang Festival and Jindo Arirang Festival on the screen. There are many other Arirang festivals held in Daegu, Miryang and Seongbuk. One should recognize that people of many different regions celebrate the same theme, Arirang. This is a very uncommon phenomenon, which impresses the tourists. In order to utilize Arirang festivals as a tourism attraction, they should implement several tactical plans.

Firstly, we should define the Arirang spirit. We need continuous financial support for professionals and experts of Arirang in order to maintain the tradition and the quality of Arirang festivals. Secondly, we should encourage the local people is sponsorship of their local Arirang festivals. This sponsorship would promote the local tradition and heritage of their Arirang. Thirdly, Arirang festivals at different localities must have a common theme with their own uniqueness.

Implementing these strategies is considered useful because Korea is expecting to host many upcoming international events such as the 2011 Daegu IAAF World Championships in Athletics, EXPO 2012(Yeosu) and the 2014 Incheon Asian Games. Arirang has played a critical role in international events before. Arirang was used to cheer the Korean soccer team in the 2002 FIFA World Cup. The Korean government also tactically deploys the Arirang music when they introduce Korea to foreign visitors. I anticipate that the Unified South-North Korea team will choose the Arirang as the team song someday. I expect a new version of Arirang will be born before and after the international events mentioned above.

Arirang has demonstrated the Korean spirit of bravery, the love of peace and patience. I believe people, regardless of their nationality, would easily find a universal appeal in Arirang. Thus, Koreans have to be equipped with viable strategies to exploit Arirang as a channel to introduce Korea to the world. One approach to present Korea to the world is gathering scattered Arirang Festivals at one place. This tactic would merge both uniqueness and similarities among different Arirang Festivals. The magnitude of such an event should be nationwide. Yuki Matsuri in Japan and Carnival in Brazil are examples that envision. The nationwide Arirang Festival should include local performers to show their own unique cultural properties to the world.

4. Sharing Arirang Culture with the World

Reviewing Arirang history would intuitively help us to appreciate its role in Korean culture and ideology. Arirang came to Koreans merely as a local folksong a century ago. Arirang was born during the restoration of Gyeongbokgung Palace (1865~1868). The workers used to sing at work. There may be many explanations why they sang Arirang while working. The most plausible one would be that they sang to ease their agony being away from family.

Arirang soon became very popular among the construction workers and the locals around the palace. Professional musicians added different flavors to Arirang. Additional change in Arirang might have occurred when those construction workers returned to their hometowns. The history of Arirang resulted in different versions of local Arirang.

Arirang was first introduced to Americans in 1896 by H. B. Hulbert, a missionary. Arirang went through turmoil and despair of Korea such as during the Japanese occupation. For example, "Ariranggogae" appearing in the verse of Arirang implies the loss and the separation of loved ones and their strength enduring their agony. Also, Arirang was popular as a theme of plays, films, pop music and dancing during the Japanese occupation. Arirang was deeply embedded in Korean people who left Korea during the Japanese occupation.

Thus, Arirang earned the honor to be called the folksong of Korea after Korea was liberated from Japan. Different events in Korea made Arirang a world song. When the Korean War broke out in 1950, UN soldiers from 16 different countries fought on South Korea's side. These soldiers learn Arirang and took it with them to their home countries. Additionally, many Koreans immigrated to Germany during 1960-70 searching for jobs. They spread Arirang to European countries. The 1986 Asian Games and 1988 Seoul Olympic Games made Arirang even more popular. The fact that the Unified Athletic Team of South and North Korea adopted Arirang as the team song earned Arirang worldwide fame.

It is also worthwhile to note the role of Arirang in political movements in Korea. Arirang was the Korean resistance troops' song during the Japanese occupation. An American reporter wrote a book on Kim San, who was a revolutionist. Kim San's love of Arirang fascinated both Koreans and Americans even after his untimely death. It is interesting to note that the North Korean government exploited Arirang in order to inspire North Koreans. For instance, the famous

Arirang Mass Games, a form of performing arts, has been played on many occasions. UNESCO has recognized the meaning of Arirang. The organization initiated the Arirang Award to honor the importance of cultural preservation. Through these socio-historical, cultural and political associations Arirang has become a precious cultural property of Korea, as well as of the world.

Arirang with its rich history also, led Koreans to develop spiritual codes unique to them. These are 1) resilience against adversity, 2) aspiration for unity and harmony and 3) desire to live in peace. I believe these Arirang spirits will play a pivotal role in the reunification process of Korea and the world peace movement as it did throughout Korean history.

The characteristics and the history of Arirang will let all Koreans in the Korean Peninsula and 147 foreign countries accept Arirang as the song of Korea. Such a national consensus is not very common in other fields. Korea has been a victim of frequent foreign invasions. Because of this, Koreans long for peace. The desire for peace can be found in Arirang as discussed previously. We should strive to share the Arirang ideology with the people of the world to establish a long lasting peace.

In a sense, some people around the world already knew it through Arirang. For example, Pearl S. Buck cited the spirits of Arirang to illustrate Korean resilience and humanism in her novel *The Living Reed*. Castro, the former president of Cuba

The Song of Ariran by Nym Wales, then acclaimed Kim San as "a new human species." Also, Oe Kenzaburo, a Nobel Prize winner in Literature and life-peace movement activist in Japan, cited Arirang story to illustrate the significance of the life-peace movement. The stories and events show that Arirang is a key concept in the life-peace movement. I believe Arirang is not only a song but also a message of humanism.

I hope I can share the significant role of Arirang with Koreans and with world citizens. I am certain that all Koreans in both South and North are proud of the song of Arirang. Eventually, the Arirang spirit can be extended to other countries for the perseverance of peace. Let me recall the theme of the most recent DMZ Arirang Festival: "The unification of heart, people and land through Arirang!"

I would like to sum up my 5 years of Arirang research as follows: "Arirang is a universal communication tool. Therefore, it is worthwhile to cherish and appreciate the Arirang tradition and spirit."

aa. Thinking Arirangology through Geography

Arirang is famously known for its beautiful melody. But to bring Arirang into greater prominence in the world, and to be able to say, "This is Arirang of our people", there is an urgent need for field of Arirangology. Experts from the fields of music, culture, history, geography, folklore, anthropology, philosophy, psychology, sociology, politics, esthetics, and many others need to come together to piece together the full story of Arirang. It is not the task for one field or one man, nor for a few fields and a few men. A comprehensive approach encompassing all related fields is required, as advocated by E. O. Wilson in his studies of consilience, to gather the knowledge and insight from each field to define a field of Arirangology.

The folksong Arirang differs in lyrics and melody depending on the singer, the region it is being sung, the climate, and the environment. If the various elements and conditions are considered and synthesized consiliently, putting heads together to discuss the definition of an Arirangology, I believe an answer may perhaps be reached.

We must reject the method of study wherein each person uses the knowledge from his own field of study to claim that he has described the Arirang fully. When the different fields work together to reveal their knowledge and insight objectively, such findings can be integrated to form a field of Arirangology that manages to reveal its true form.

On December 14, 2011, International Conference for Arirang was held in Seoul, Korea. In the keynote speech by chairman Cho Dong-il, he said that they should approach and affirm Arirangology as a "radical science". He even quoted from a book of mine, A Geographer's, Arirang Journey, saying "Geography is Arirang" and "History is Arirang".

In my book, I claimed that it is necessary to refer to E. O.

Wilson's concept of consilience to the study of Arirang in order to define a field of Arirangology. I believe that the "radical science" that chairman Cho proposed is in full agreement with E. O. Wilson's concept of consilience.

Subsequently, our folksong, the Arirang, cannot be studied by any one man or any one field. Many people from many fields must participate to perform a multilateral and comprehensive analysis to establish a definition of Arirangology. There is no shortcut or a final destination. Only by putting our heads together and continuing our research can we achieve our final objective.

Reference

■ Books & Essays

Ahnno Mitsumasa(2001) *The Landscape of a Song*, Tokyo: Kodansha, P.66.

Akiba Noboru(1954.7) *Korean Folklore*, Tokyo: Rokusan Shoin, pp.245-249

Allen, Horace N.(1908) Things Korean, Fleming H. Revell Company, pp.55-56.

Ahn Byeong-seop(1988) "Na Un-gyu's Film Arirang", Korean Journal 28(7), pp.48-51.

Ahn Ji-dam (1930) Ancient and Modern of Folksong in Korea, Seoul: Joseon Vol.14 No.5, pp.31-40.

Annals of the Joseon Dynasty (1817) Sunjo 17 yrs. The Original No. 46, p.415.

Atkins E. Taylor (2007) The Dual Career of "Arirang" : The Korean Resistance Anthem that became a Japanese Pop Hit, *The Journal of Asian Studies*. Vol.66. No3. August, pp. 645-687.

Baek Dae-bong(2004) *The Other Side and Consensus of the Traditional Music*, Seoul: Jisik Sanup Publishing Co, pp.289-292.

Bang Sang-hyun et al(1993) Korean Migration History in Russia, Seoul: Tamgudang, pp.11-13.

Bishop, Isabella Bird(1831-1904) (1898) *Korea and Her Neighbors*, London: Kegan Paul, pp.165-168.

Brandt Kim(2000) "Objects of Desire: Japanese Collections and Colonial Korea.", Positions : *East Asia Cultures Critique* 8(3), pp.711-746.

Choi Chang-ho(2003) folksong Journey : Samcheolli, Pyongyang : Pyongyang Publishing Company, pp.54-60, 119-121.

Cheon In-pyong(1968) Music of Central Asia and Korea, *Essays in Musicology*, National Classical Music Society, pp.359-424.

Cheon Yi-doo(1985) *Korean Literature and Grudge*, Seoul: IU Publish, p.34.

Cheon Yi-doo(1987) The Structure of Han of Korea(in Japanese), Tokyo: *Samcheolli*. Feb. No. 49.

Cheon Yi-doo(1989) On Korea's grudge - with reference to Japanese Monono Aware, Chosengakuho, No. 131, pp.95-113.

Cho Dong-il(1980) The Meaning and Function of Personal Legend, Daegu: Yeungnam University Press, pp.75-76.

Choi Gil-seong(1988) The Image of the Traditional Women in Conjunction with the Grudge, Sejong Language and Literature(16 and 17), pp.678-697.

Choi Gil-seong(1988) The Symobolic Meaning of Grudge-with Reference to the Death of General Choe Yeong, Seoul: Comparative Folklore No. 4, pp.39-48, 63-67.

Choi Gil-seong(1991) *The Love and Hate of Koreans*, Seoul: Yejinsa, pp.13-15.

Choi Yeong-han(1932) *Theory of the Korean Folksong*, Donggwang Vol 4 No.5. Donggwangsa, p.132.

Choi Yeong-ju(1984) A Study of Comparative and Analysis on the Transformation of Bonjo Arirang, Gwangju: Chosun University, College of Education. Music major, pp.8-20.

Chung Dong-hwa(1981) A Historical Research of the Folksong of Korea, Seoul: Iljogak, p.48.

Chung Dong-hwa(1983) *Korean's Consciousness Structure Appearing in the Folksong*, Seoul: Korea Broadcasting Industrial Co, pp.111-137.

Darisa(1971) The Song of Arirang. *Monthly Darisa*, Seoul: Darisa, pp.164-167.

Donga Color Encyclopedia(1982) No.28 p.54.

Frisby W. and D. Gotz(1989) "Festival Management: A Case Study Perspective", Journal of Travel Research 28(1), pp.7-11.

Fujii Hajime(1981) Tango. Heibonsha's World Encyclopedia Vol. 19, Tokyo: Heibonsha, p.498.

Fukuji Hiroaki(1992) *The Women in the Battle of Okinawa- A group of Korean Women Entertainers for Japanese Soldiers*, Tokyo: Kaifusha, pp.12, 45-54.

Fursyth James(1992) translated by Chung Jae K, *A History of the Peoples of Siberia: North Asian Colony* 1581-1990, London : Colombia University Press, p.325.

Griffiths A. Paul(1978) *A Concise History of Modern Music*, The World Art Library, London: Thames and Hudson, p.124.

Griffis William Elliot(1905) *Corea. The Hermit Nation*, London: Harpe and Brothers, pp.212-213.

Hamaguchi Yosemitsu(1927) The Flavor of the Folksong in Korea. Choe Nam-seon edited. *The Study of Korean Folksong*, Seoul: Jinsimsa, pp.13-17.

Han Chang-dong(1984) The Mood of the Folksong in My Hometown, Pyeongan-do Province Part, p.213.

Han Man-young(1973) A Study on the Mode of Folksong in the Eastern Part of Mt.Taebaeksan : *The Collection of Papers on Arts*, Seoul: Yesulwon, p.141.

Han Man-young(1991) The Mode of Folksong in the Eastern Part of Mt. Taebaeksan. A Study of Traditional Music in Korea, Seoul: Pungnam Publishing Company, pp.171-189.

Han Yang-myeong(1989) An Approach on the Legend of Jindo Arirang, Korean Folklore No.22, p.138.

Han Yang-myeong(2001) A Study of Arirang Taryeong. The Collection of Folklore Scientific Materials in Korea, Seoul: Noraemadangteo, pp.373, 443, 456-460, 462-468.

Han Yu-han(1941) Amnokgang March, Composer Han Yu-han and Lyric writing Park Young-man from Park Chan-ho(1987) The History of Korean Ballad, Tokyo: Shobunsha, pp.59-60.

Hinnengan, R(1977) *Oral Poetry*, London: Cambridge University Press, p.29.

Hong Sa-joung(1977) A Sorrowful Tune of the Song of Arirang and National Character, Seoul: Dongseomunhwa, p.57.

Hosokawa Shuhei(1998) "In Search of the Sound of Empire: Tanabe Hisao and the Foundation of Japanese Ethnomusicology", *Japanese Studies* 18(1):5-19.

Howard Keith(1986) "Korea's Intangible Cultural Properties: A Review of the 16th Festival of Human Cultural Properties", *Korean Journal* 26(1), pp.61-68.

Howard Keith(2001) "Korean Folksong for a Contemporary World." In Contemporary Directions: *Korean Folkmusic Engaging the twentieth Century and Beyond*, ed. Nathan Hesselink, pp.149-72. Berkely, California: Institute of East Asian Studies

Hulbert, H. B.(1906) *The Passing of Korea(Joseon yugi)*, pp.314-329.

Hwang Yu-bok(2002) *Re-lighting of the Korean Society in China*, Romyeong: Minjok Publishing Company, pp.21-23.

Im Dong-gwon(1974) *A Study of the Folksong of Korea*, Seoul: Seonmyeong Munhwasa, pp.73-74.

Im Seock-Jae(2004) *The Collection of an Oral Narrative Korean Folksong*, The Academy of Korean Studies, Seoul: Minsokwon, pp.6-9.

Im Yeong-sang, Hwang, Yeong-nam et al(2005) *The Society of Kareiski and Its Change and Korean People*, Seoul: Hankuk University of Foreign Studies Press, pp.193-226.

Im Yeong-sang(2012) *Goreyin Shinseowon*, Seoul pp.166-169.

Imamura Domo(1928) *Historical Folklore of the Comic Chat of Korea*, Seoul: Nanshan Ginsha, p.410.

Ishikawa Giichi(1923) The Relationship between Korean Music and Curve of the Mountain, Chosun, pp.135-137.

Ishinara Shintaro(2004) Japanese Suicide Squad - Admirable Imagine of Young Group, Tokyo: Bungeishunshusha, pp.94-98.

Itagaki Ryuta(2004) Revisiting "Colonial Modernity": The Present State and Issues in Korean Historiography, Rekishi horn, 654:35-45.

Ichiyama Morio(1927) *The Study of Korean Folksong*, Tokyo: Sakamoto Shoten, pp.70-75, 116-124.

Ito Takashi(1997) Kim, Mun-gyu Translated. The Song of Arirang in Sakhalin, Seoul: Sulebakyu, collection 2. NoonBitts, pp.203-204.

Itsuki Hiroyuki(2007) *The Journey to Visit the Korea's Buddhist Temples-in 21st Century*, Tokyo: Kodansha. pp.193.

Janelli Roger R.(1986) "The Origin of Korean Folksong Scholarship", *Journal of American Folklore* 99, pp.24-99.

Jang Deouk-sun et al(1979) The Essay of the Oral Literature, Seoul: Iljogak, p.75.

Jang Joon-hee(2004) Search for Oases in Continental Central Asia Chung-A Seoul, p.321-350.

Jang Sa-hun and Han Man-young(1975) Jeongseon Arirang the Introduction of Naturnal Music. Seoul: Seoul National University Press, p.238.

Jang Sa-hun and Seong Gueong-lin(1949) The Folksong of Korea Seoul: International Music and Culture Company, p.213.

Jeong Beom-tae(2002) *Noted Person, and Master Singer*, Seoul: Gipeunsaem, P.93.

Jeong Hun-mo(1965) Ahn Eaktai Observed by a Vocalist-Jeong, Hun-mo. *Music Life Vol. 1*, Seoul: The Music Research Institute of Korea, pp.170-171.

Jeong Jae-ho(1984) *A Complete Collection of the Popular Song of Korea*, Seoul: Semyeong Munhwasa, p.20.

Jeong Mock-il(essay), Shin Byung-cheol(photo)(2005) *Seventy seven Beaties in*

Korea(Arirang included), Seoul: Segyemunye, p.205.

Jeongseon(2003) *Jeongseon Arirang*, p.13.

Ji Chun-sang and Na Gyeong-su(1988) The Essay on the Formation of the Song of Jindo Arirang. *Research Institute of Honam Culture. Vol.18*, Gwangju: Research Institute of Honam Culture at Chonnam National University, p.31, 65.

Jin Yong-seon(2000) Korea's Arirang in China, Seoul: Sumoon Publishing Company, p.44.

Jin Yong-seon(2004) Jeongseon Arirang. Gangwon-do Study Series 3, Seoul: Jipmoondang, p.4.

Jo Jeong-rae(1994) *Arirang Roman Fleuve*, Seoul: Hainaim, pp.211-232

Jo U-hwa(1984) Arirang, Seoul: Dongnyeok Munye(Kim San and Nym Wales, pp. 297-300.

Ju Dae-Chang(2003) Evaluation of Musical Skill of Jindo Arirang Observed by the Musical Technique, Seoul: World Muisical Society, pp.55-79.

Ju Wang-san(1947.10) *Introduction of the Folksong of Korea*, Seoul: Dongyang Print Copy, p.6.

Jun Dae-wan(2011) Do you know about Uzbekistan? Seoul, Hwanam pp.54-67, 76-79.

Jung Pal-yong(2011) Arirang of North Korea, International Conference for Arirang, Seoul, pp.154-158.

Jung Pal-yong(2011) *Arirang of North Korea*, International Conferance for Arirang, Seoul, p.159-160.

Kang Deung-hak(1988) *A Study of Jeongseon Arari*, Seoul: Jipmoondang, pp.11-14, 25-32, 193-195.

Kang In-cheol(1998) Neverthless Koreans are still managing their lives, Haein, pp.29-30.

Karashima Takeshi(1942) The Current Phase of Culture Policy in Korea *Chosun*, pp.4-20.

Kawata Tadashi(1965) *Tadao Yanainara and International Pacifism*, Tokyo: Chuokoron, p.437.

Kim B. Hee(2010) A Study on Korean Diaspora' s Arirang Songs with Reference to North Korea and Soviet Union: Symposium: Today and Tomorrow of Arirangology in Korea Research Center for Art and Literature of Korea: Soongsil University. PP.113-130

Kim Byung-ha, Kim Yeon-gap(1996) Jeongseon Arirang, Seoul: Beomwoosa, p.5.

Kim Chan-sam(1962) The Endless Journey (A) Seoul: Eomungak, p.114, also see The Endless Journey(B), Seoul: Eomungak, p.163, 167, 350.

Kim Chong-wook(1980) This is an Original Text on the Film of Arirang, Seoul: *Screen*, p.66.

Kim Chong-wook(2002) Chunsa Na Woonkyu' s Complete Works Material Collection, pp.39-46.

Kim Dae-haeng(1995) The Types of a Seductive Tones of a Korean Poem, Lyric Lines, Dance Music, Korean Traditional Narrative Songs, and Folksong. Study of Koreanology vol. 7, a Institute of Koreanology, Korea University.

Kim Dae-haeng(2008) *The World Wide Values of the Song of Jeongseon Arirang*, pp.14-24.

Kim Gi-hyeon(2001) The Formation Period of the Song of Arirang. *The Thesis Collection of Folksong*. No. 6, Seoul: Minsonkwon, pp.21-42.

Kim Gi-hyeon(1955) The Formation Process and Structure of Miryang Arirang Thesis Collection of Folksong No. 4, pp.95-121.

Kim Jae-cheol(1930) On the Folksong Arirang, Chosun Ilbo, July 11th .

Kim Ji-yeon(1929) A Study of Folksong of Arirang, Magazine *Chosun* No.141.

Kim Ji-yeon(1930) A Study of Folksong of Arirang, Magazine *Chosun* No.151, 152.

Kim Ji-yeon(1930) Folksong- Arirang, *Chosun, No.152.*

Kim Kyung-Won(1995) Itsuki's Lullaby-the Relationship between Itsuki's Lullaby and the Song of Arirang, Seoul: The Collection of Folksong No.4, pp.81-92.

Kim Ryu-yeon(2010) Mr Koh Chang-soo, Dedicated His Life for the Project of the Arirang Mass Games Gumsoogangsan. pp.28-29.

Kim San, Nym Wales(1941) Song of Ariran, New York: John Day Publishing-Refer to Preface.

Kim Sa-ryang(1988) Mt, Taebaeksan-Outline of Modern Korea-A Full-length Novel 2, pp.106-130.

Kim Seon-pung(2003) On Arirang in the Korean Folklore. Korean Traditional Culture. No. 19. The Association of Korean Traditional Culture, Seoul: Sudeok Munhwasa, pp.427-436.

Kim Seong-gi(2004) Uzbekistan, Seoul: Myungsung Publishing, pp.61-63.

Kim Shi-eop(1985) *Modern Folksong: the Formation of the Characters of the Song of Arirang in the Turning Point of East Asian Literature*, Seoul: Changbi Publishers, pp.215, 245-251.

Kim Sung-bae(1976) *A Study on the Korean Buddhist Hymn-with its Historical Development*, Seoul: Asia Culture press, p.161.

Kim Tae-jun(2005) The Pass of the Song of Arirang- the Space of Mental Image of the People in the Present Age, Seoul: *The Geography of Literature*(2), pp.463-480.

Kim Yeol-gyu(1987) *The Song of Arirang: History, Korean folks, and Sound!*, Chosun Ilbo Press, pp.30-31, 96-97, 120-125, 321.

Kim Yeon-gap(1988) "The Origin of Arirang and Meari as its Original Form", *Korean Journal 28(7)*, pp.20-34.

Kim Yeon-gap(1989) *The Song of Arirang: its Flavor, and Taste, and⋯*, Seoul: Jipmoondang, pp.132.

Kim Yeon-gap(1994) *The Arirang Journey with reference to all Korea*, Seoul:

Jipmoondang, pp.296-298.

Kim Yeon-gap(2000) Grudge in Korean Literature and the Song of Arirang, *Farmers Literature*, vol.59, pp.34-37.

Kim Yeon-gap(2002) A Study of Folk-songs of North Korea, Seoul: Cheong Song Publishing, pp.307-334.

Kim Yeon-gap(2006) A Study of Theories related to the Song of Arirang, Seoul: Myeong Sang, pp.369-370.

Kim Yeon-gap(2012) Ki Meeyang(translator) The Culture of Arirang, Seoul: Jipmoondang, pp.243-249.

Kim Yeon-su(1989) The Undisclosed History of Korean in USSR enforced Migration in Central Asia, *Korea Journal for East-West European Studies vol.4. No.1*, pp.147-156.

Kim Yeon-su(1990) Korean People Victimized by the Stalin's Terror Politics: The Disclosed History of the Forced Korean Migration into Central Asia, *Monthly Yeoksa Sanchaek No. 3*. Seoul: Beomunsa, pp.28-31, 36.

Kim Yeong-jun(1994) *Tale of the Folksong History* of Korea, Seoul: Arum Publising Company, pp.225.

Kim Sun-nam(1982) *Sailor's Song of Korea*, Seoul: Hoaksa, pp.16-17.

Kishibe Shigeo(1980) "China, Court Traditions" *The New Grove Dictionary of Music and Musicians. ed. Stanely Sadie. Vol. IV*, London: MacMillan Publishers Limited, p.250.

Koga Masao(1932) Song of Arirang: On Korean Folksong, Kaizo, December, pp.87-89.

Kolaiz W.(1954) The People of the Soviet Far East, New York, pp.38-39.

Koh Jeong-ok(1949) *A study of Folksong of Korea*, Seoul: Suseonsa, p.15.

Koh Suk-gyeong(1980) A Study on Jeongseon Arirang, Seoul: Graduate School of Kyung Hee University, Music Department, Major in Vocal Music, pp.5-33.

Kondodokki, Ghas(1929) *A Historical Tale and Myth. Noticed Visited in Korea*,

Seoul: Bakmungak, pp.22-27.

Kusano Taeko(1984) *The Song of Arirang: In Search of the Fascinating Korean Traditional Music*, Tokyo: Hakusuisha, pp.130-131, 192, 211, 247.

Kwon O-seong(1982) Arirang. *Donga Encyclopedia Vol. 19*, Seoul: Donga Publishing Company, pp.346.

Kwon O-seong(2006) *Korea's Tranditional Music*, Seoul: Minsoksa, pp.463-464.

Leach, MacEdward, ed(1975) *The Ballad Book*, New York: A. S. Barnes and Company, p.42.

Lee Bo-hyeong(1988) "Musical Study on Arirang", *Korea Journal* 28(7):35-47.

Lee Beom-seung The Living Status of Korean Farmers who Settled in Kanto, China. *Chosun Vol. 14. No.9*, pp.64.

Lee Chung-myun(1961) *Recent Population Patterns and Trends of the Republic of Korea*, Ann Arbor, Michigan. pp.119-129.

Lee Chung-myun(1987) Vestiges of Korean Migration into the Sanin and Hokuriku Region in Ancient Japan, *Journal of Geography*. vol. 14 Seoul National University, pp.229-247.

Lee Chung-myun(1999) *Asian Americans in Utah* (Korean Part). Compiled by John H. Yang. Living History. Salt Lake City: The State of Utah Office of Asian Affairs. *The Asian American Advisory Council*, pp. 140-174.

Lee Chung-myun(2007) A Geographer's Arirang Journey, Seoul: Easy Puhlishing Co. pp.55-58.

Lee Chung-myun(2009) *Arirang : Song of Korea*, Seoul: Easy Publishing Co. pp.99-147.

Lee Chul-u(2012.11) A Some Consideration of Song of Arirang of Korea, Monograph, Tokyo, pp.1-14.

Lee Gwang-su(1924) A Consideration of Korean Folksong. *Literature and Critique*, pp.52-53.

Lee Gwang-su(1927) One Aspect of the Korean People appeared in the Folksong of Korea. *A Study of the Folksong of Korea*, Seoul: Seongjin

Munhwasa. pp.70-75.

Lee Gyu-tae(1978) *Was the Song of Arirang the Name of the Pass?-A Different View- History of Korea*, Seoul: Wooil Munhwasa, p.200.

Lee Gyu-tae(1989) *Arirang: Koreanology*, Seoul: Girin Seonwon, pp.23-24, 201-202.

Lee Hye-ku(1966-4) What is Buddist Hymn *Religious Circle, No.3*, pp.178-183

Lee Jae-wu(1998) Romantics During the Age of Sailing Vessels and the Song Filled with Love and Hate. *The Ocean of Korea*, Jeonnam: Mokpo National Maritime University, pp.251-253.

Lee Jeong-nan(1988) Shaman Music in Jindo Island, *Nationl Folk Museum of Korea*, p.77, 89.

Lee Jin-seop(1965) Search for Chanson-Paris and Common People' s Consanguinity. *Music Life Vol. 1*, Seoul: The Music Research for Korea, pp.190-192.

Lee Jin-won(2002) The Comparative Approach to Korean Arirang and Chinese Arari. *The History of Korean Music No. 29*, Seoul: The Association of Music History in Korea, pp.597-612.

Lee O-young(1982) *The Mind of Korean People, Revised the Theory of Civilization of the Love and Hate*, Tokyo: Haksaengsa, pp.267-268.

Lee Seok-chan(1931) The Status of the Ethnical Koreans in the Manchuria, China, Seoul: Shinhak Jinamsa, p.402.

Lee Yo-seop(2007) *The Journey of World Folksong*, Seoul: Yeyeong Communication, pp.51-53.

Machida Kasho and Asano, Kenchi ed.(1960) *The Folksong of Japan*, Tokyo: Iwanami Bunko, pp.21-23, 362-363, 509-511.

Machida Kasho(2005) *Japanese Folksong*, Tokyo: Iwanami Shoten, pp.510-511

McCann, David R.(1979) Arirang: The National Folksong of Korea, In Studies on Korea in Tradition. *Occasional Papers No. 9*, ed. David R. McCann, John Middleton, and Edward J. Shultz, Honolulu: Center for Korean Studies, University of Hawaii, pp.45-46.

Michi Hisa Ryo(1927) The Life of the Shifting Cultivator and Their Song. *A Study of Folksong of Korea*(Choe Nam-seon ed), Seoul: Seongjin Munhwasa, pp.109-115.

Mikado Amagaje(1965) Itsuki's Lullaby. *The Encycolpedia of Japanese Folksong. No. 1*. Symphony Music Score Publisher, p.46.

Mayatsuka Toshio(1995) *The Re-birth of Arirang-the Soul of Korean People Engraved in the Song*, Tokyo: Sochisa, pp.178-180, 288-289.

Moon Chung-ho(2009) A Study on the Identity of the Ethnical Koreans in Central Asia.

Moon Song-yop(2003) Journal of Social Science Academy, Editing board of Social Sciences Publisher, p.51-56. The Origin and Variation of Korean People(2), p.35-39.

Murakami Masamichi(2005) Arirang-Itsuki's Lullaby is Arirang, *Rebirth-Lullaby!*, *Tokyo*: Fujihara Shoten, pp.154-155.

Nakano Seiichi(1913) Yalu River Journey-North West Border Region in North Korea, Chosengakuho, No.131.

Na Su-bu(1996) *The Song of Arirang made the Beautiful Land of Korea Cry*, Seoul: Dongmyeong Publishing Company, pp.107-109, 226-238.

Na Un-gyu (1930) The Arirang Society and I. Samcheolli July, Seoul: Samcheollisa, pp.53-54

Nam Hye-gyeong et al.(2005) *The Kareiski Human Migration and Economic Environment*, Seoul: Jipmoondang, pp.9-11, 32-34, 141-147.

Noh Dong-eun(1989) *The Present Stage of Korean Music*, Seoul: Segwang Music Publisher, pp.39-56.

Oh Yeong-hee(1995) The Treatment of the Love and Hate by Way of Forgiveness: with Reference to the Psychological Approach, *The Korean Journal of Counseling and Psychotherapy*. Vol. 7 No.1, pp. 70-94.

Park Byeong-hun ed(1986) Jindo Arirang Taryeong, Jindo: Jindo Cultural

Center, p.14.

Park Chan-ho(1989) The History of Korean Ballad, Tokyo: Shobunsha, pp.152-63.

Park Gwan-su(2005) A Study on the Diffusion of the Folksong in Gangwon-do Province, Lee Bo-hyeong et al.(2005) *The Folksong of Gangwon and the Spot of Livelyhood*, Gangwon-do: The Developtment of Research Institute in Gangwon-do Province, pp.89-120.

Park Gyeong-shik(2005) *The Record on the Enforced Korean Laborers*, Tokyo: Miraisha, pp.20-22, 169.

Park Gyeong-su(1995) The Result and Task of Folksong Study, *The Collection of Folksong 4*, pp.323-347.

Park Heon-bong(1965) The Position of the Folklore Music in the Cultural History. *Cultural Properties First Edition*, Seoul: The Bureau of the Cultural Heritage Administration. p.92.

Park I-jeong(1998) A Study of Folksong History. *The Folklore Society Ed*, p.97

Park Jeong-se(1986) A Study of the Essence of the Love and Hate(grudge) Appeared on the Myth of a Victim. *The 14th National Announce*, pp.489-494.

Park Min-il(1957) A Study on Pro-Japanese 'Arirang', *The Collection of Folksong of the Association of Folksong in Korea Vol. 5*, Seoul: Minsokwon, pp.305-309.

Park Min-il(2002) *The History of Arirang Mentality*, Kangnung-Wonju University Press, p.55.

Park Sang-gyu(2001) A Study about Commonness for Folksong between Korea and Mongolia. *The Collection of Folksong Vol. 6*, Seoul: The Association of Folksong in Korea, pp.155.

Park Sang-yeoul(1991) *Jindo Arirang*, Seoul: Hangilsa, pp.38-39.

Park Tae-bong(2004) *The inside Story and Sympathy of Traditional Music in Korea*, Seoul: Knowledge Industrial Company, pp.289-292.

Pema Gyalpo(2005) Thinking of Peace through Lullaby. *Rebirth Lullaby!* Tokyo: Fujiwara Shoten, p.218.

Rouseau J. J. *World Encyclopedia Vol. 14*, Tokyo: Heibonsha, pp.192-194.

Rutt Richard(1965) *Graceful Korea*, Seoul: Shintaeyang, pp.18-23.

Ryang Sonia(1997) "Japanese Travelers' Accounts of Korea." E*ast Asian History*, No.13: 133-52.

Sato Katsumi(2004.1) The Tragedy of the Return Home Campaign of North Korean is: Special Plan Father Teaches to Son-History of Showa Period. After War edition 20, Tokyo: *Bungei Shunshu*, pp.318-320.

Schmid Andre(1997) Rediscovering Manchuria: Shin Chae-ho and the Politics of Territorial History in Korea, *Journal of Asian Studies 56(1)*, pp.26-46.

Schmid Andre(2000) Colonialism and the Korea Problem' in the Historiography of Modern Japan, *Journal of Asian Studies 59(4)*, pp.951-76.

Seo Dae-suk(1987) *Koreans in the Soviet Union*, Hawaii, p.88.

Seo Jeong-beom(1980) *Shamanism in Korea*, Tokyo: Dohosha, pp.172-173.

Shin Heung-U(1938) The Benefactor of Korea-H.B. Hulbert, *The First Edition of Samcheonli*, pp.14-15.

Shinobu Junpei(1901) *Korean Peninsula*, Tokyo: Tokyodo Shoten, pp.106-107

Takahashi Tohoru(1932) Korean Folksong, *Chosun. No.201*, pp.15-19.

Takahashi Tohoru(1933) *The Folksong of North Korea* (in Japanese), Chosun, No.219, pp.356-357.

Tanabe Hisao(1930) Court Music. *Nippon Chiri Daikei. Vol. 16*, Tokyo: Shinkosha, pp.187.

Tanabe Hisao(1971) Ancient Japan and Korea Observing Throughout Music, *Nipono Nakano Chosun Bunka 12*, Kyoto: Nipono Nakano Chosun Bunkasha, pp.4-10.

Tanabe Hisao(1972) Ancient Japan and Korea Observing Throughout Music, *Nipono Nakano Chosun Bunka 12*, Kyoto: Nipono Nakano

Chosun Bunkasha, pp.60-65.

Tanabe Hisao(1973) The Question on the Komakaku in Japan. *Nipono Nakano Chosun Bunka 18*, Kyoto: Nipono Nakano Chosun Bunkasha, pp.41-45.

Tanabe Hisao(1981) Arirang. Heibonsha's World Encyclopedia vol.1, Tokyo: Heibonsha, pp.478.

United Nations(Ed)(1951) International Migrations in the Far East during Times Population Bulletin New York, p.27.

Won Hun-ui(1988) A study of the lyric of Jeongseon Arirang. *Gwandong Hyangto Munhwa No.2*, p.112.

Yamada Shyoji(1977) The Arirang Pass in Tsukuho-The Survey of Focused on the Enforced Korean Labor Recruitment, pp.22-34.

Yamamoto Makiko(1970) *World Tour-South Amerca*, Tokyo: Kawade Shobo, pp.57-58.

Yanaihara Tadao(1924) *Colony of Korea and the Colonization Policy*, Tokyo: Yuhikaku, p.379.

Yanaihara Tadao(1927) *The New Bases for the Colonial Policy*, Kyoto: Hobun Shobo, pp.329-336.

Yang Byung-soon(2009) Koreiski, Kazakhstan, Korean Story, Seoul: Guidepost Publishing, p.235.

Yi Byung-do(1956) The Legend of the Song of 'Arirang'. Dugye's *Miscellaneous*, Seoul: Iljogak, pp.31-33.

Yi So-ra(2001) A Consideration of the Song of Arirang and Its Origin, Seoul: Minsokwon, pp.303-320.

Yi So-ra(1998) The Propagation and Change of Folksong Essays in Musicology. An Offering in celebration of Lee Hye-ku on his Ninetieth Birthday *Eassays in Musicloy*, Seoul: National Classical Music Society, pp.325-344.

Uemura Yukio(2011) An Arirang Hypothesis of the Origin of 'Itsukino

Komoriutah' (A Lulluby of Itsuki Village), International Conference for Arirang, Seoul, pp.220-222.

Uhm Ha-jin(1992) The Origin of Folksongs in Korea, Pyongyang Yesul Kyoyuk Publishing Company, pp.112-113, 189-193.

Uno Yusuke(2005) The Kinds of Locality of Lullabies Robirth of lullaby.

Uno Yusuke(1996) A Study on Social Background of the Lullaby in Jukoku Region. *Research Bulletin of Tottori Women's College. No. 33*, pp.79-80.

Yamane Ginzo, others(1952) *Music and Politics, Music Art 10*(6) Ongakuno Tomosha Tokyo. pp.11-20

Yun Su-dong(2000) *Choson Minyo 1000 gokgip*, Pyongyang Munhakyesul Publishing. Reserch Materials, p.364, p.612.

Yun Su-dong(2003) On Minyo 'Changsangot Taryong', Pyongyang Yesul Kyoyuk Publishing Company, p.76.

Yun Su-dong(2011) Arirang Folksong of Korea Literature, Pyongyang Yesul Kyoyuk Publishing Company, pp.26-46, 55-60.

■ Newspapers

Chosun Ilbo(1924.11.27) Observing Drama-Arirang Pass. Drama Review.

Chosun Ilbo(1927. 10.27) Arirang Censor.

Chosun Ilbo(1927. 7. 12) The Structure of the Song of Arirang.

Chosun Ilbo(1929.11.26) Seeing the Arirang gogae show Performed by Towolhoe.

Chosun Ilbo(1930.7.11) Jeongseon Arari.

Chosun Ilbo(1930.11.18) Personal View of Folksong.

Chosun Ilbo(1931. 7.11) On the folksong. Kim Jae-cheol.

Chosun Ilbo(1933.1.10) Lee Aerisu as Best Singer of the Song of Arirang.

Chosun Ilbo(1934.3.27) The Introduction of the Folksong of Korea-part of the Folksong. Kim Tae-jun.

Chosun Ilbo(1934.5.11) Confiscated Richard Choi's Records.

Chosun Ilbo(1935.2.6) Migrants cross over the Yalu River on and on.

Chosun Ilbo(1935. 2. 19) Yeongcheon Arirang, Hong Jong-in, Journalist.

Chosun Ilbo(1935. 7.14) Jindo Arirang well received by the Audience.

Chosun Ilbo(1935. 12.19) Yeongcheon Arirang. Hong Jong-in.

Chosun Ilbo(1938.10.23) Germany's Marathon Symphony.

Chosun Ilbo(1938.11.26) Report on the First Motion Picture Festival.

Chosun Ilbo(1939.6.5) Shin Il-seon's Unhappy Life.

Chosun Ilbo(1939.6.19) The Heart Broken Song of Gangwon-do Arirang.

Chosun Ilbo(1939.8.14) Arang and Miryang. Chung Kwang-hyun.

Chosun Ilbo(1940.1.9) Came from Wonsan, Korea Sung the Song of Arirang
    at Japanese Theater. Kim An-la.

Chosun Ilbo(1945.12.9) The Heart Broken Song of Arirang.

Chosun Ilbo(1946.11.8) The 38 Degrees North Latitude is a New Version of
    the Pass of the Song of Arirang. Kim Hee-seung.

Chosun Ilbo(1955.4.12) A Some Consideration of the Folksong of the Orient.
    Kim Dong-jin.

Chosun Ilbo(1962.4.2) How to Upgrade the Korean Traditional Music.

Chosun Ilbo(1983.9) The Report on the Arirang Path.(A, B).

Chosun Ilbo(1985.10.31) The Story of H.B. Hulbert.

Chosun Ilbo(1988.3.5, 3.6, 3.16) I Observed the USSR-the Change of Status
    since Gorbachyov Appeared.

Chosun Ilbo(2000. 7.12) Structure of the Song of Arirang.

Chosun Ilbo(2011. 10. 12) Arirang Specialist(South Korea) Visit North Korea.

Dong-a Ilbo(1926.10.17) The Introduction of Actress Shin Il-seon.

Dong-a Ilbo(1927.3.30) Shijo(a Kind of Short Lyric), Folksong. Yeom Sang-
    seop.

Dong-a Ilbo(1928. 11.15) A Story of Korean Folksong Presented by the

Columbia Company.

Dong-a Ilbo(1932.9.19) Koga Masao's Song of Arirang.

Dong-a Ilbo(1936.4.15) Beyond the Pacific Ocean There were singing the Korea's Folksong-Arirang Pass.

Dong-a Ilbo(1936.1.1) Report on Excellent Performance of the Song by Nagata Genjiro(Kim Young-kil).

Dong-a Ilbo(1937.9.2) A Study of Korean Folksong(1). Kim Sa-yeop.

Dong-a Ilbo(1937.9.3) A Study of Korean Folksong(2). Kim Sa-yeop.

Dong-a Ilbo(1937.9.7) A Study of Korean Folksong(3). Kim Sa-yeop.

Dong-a Ilbo(1937.11.21) The Hearbreaking Song-Jeongseon Arari. Yeom Geun-su.

Dong-a Ilbo(1938. 1. 4) The Conspicuous Figures in the Field of Art.

Dong-a Ilbo(1954.4.6) The Ferewell of Youngesters Mission.

Dong-a Ilbo(1954.6.4) The Youngestars Deligation Singing the Song in Detroit.

Dong-a Ilbo(1955.5.3) A Examination of the Song of Arirang. Yang Ju-dong.

Dong-a Ilbo(1955.5.4) A Examination of the Song of Arirang. Yang Ju-dong.

Dong-a Ilbo(1960.12.23) Attending the Performance of the Court Music.

Dong-a Ilbo(1962. 4.14) Seeing the Noted Singers and Master Hands in the Mass Meeting.

Dong-a Ilbo(1972. 9. 5) Lee Myun-sang's Profile : Composer of the Opera ? Pibada and Committee Chair of the Composer's Association of North Korea.

Dong-a Ilbo(1987.8.4) Discovered the Original Copy of Arirang Related to Movie Novel.

Dong-a Ilbo(2007.5.22) Professsor Lee Chung-myun, University of Utah Published the Book Entitled, a Geographer's Arirang Journey. Lee Kwang-pyo.

Dong-a Ilbo(2007.8.14) How did They are Changing the Song of Arirang in

Japan.

Dong-a Ilbo(2007.10.31) Resound the Song of Arirang in Kumamoto Prefecture in Japan, Reader.

Dong-a Ilbo(2008.10.16) We may Listen to All the Song of Arirang in Korea at a Same Place-opening Ceremony Jeongseon Arirang Festival.

Dong-a Ilbo(2009.6.23) Yesterday and Today of the Maritine Province of Siberia Examined from the key point of Economic Development of Korea.

Dong-a Ilbo(2012.12.7) Arirang Appeared as the 'World Style', p.A15, 25.

Gumsoogangsan(2006), Hong Beom-do, p.43.

Hankyoreh(1989.8.9) Kim San's Own Children Met at Beijing.

Hankyoreh(2006.9.25) Let Spread the Song of Arirang All Over the World, Kim Chung-hwa.

JoongAng Ilbo(1965.11.2) Instrumental Music of Peasant.

JoongAng Ilbo(1984.3.17-31) I was a Group of Women Entertainers for Japanese Soldiers. Noh Su-bok.

JoongAng Ilbo(1990.7.1) Jurney with Arirang(8) Geochilhyeondong in Jeongseon. Lee Geun-bae.

JoongAng Ilbo(1994) The Sound and Vibration of the Song of Arirang Obseved from the Mt. Taebaeksan. Culture Joongang. Im Gyu-chan.

JoongAng Ilbo(2005.8.20) The Song of Arirang in Sakhalin.

JoongAng Ilbo(2007.3.8) German Cross Over the Wall Separatead Between the South and North.

JoongAng Ilbo(2008.12.12) Presented Yeongcheon Arirang to the Yeongcheon Citizens. Hwang sun-joon.

JoongAng Ilbo(2009.6.27) Kareiski problem is the Shadow of Korean History-Korean Goverment Ready to Investigate to Real Picture of Kareiski in the Central Asia.

Jaeman Choseonin Tongshin(1938) Vol 46, pp.5~6.

Korean Times of Utah(2003) The Story of Pianist(Kim Chul-woong) Escaped from North Korea. Lee Chung-myun.

Korean Times of Utah(2004) A Story of Lightning Bug-(Tak Gyeong-hyeon). Lee Chung-myun.

Korean Times of Utah(2004) Arirang Journey, Lee Chung-myun.

Korean Times of Utah(2005) Seek for the Song of Arirang (A, B, C). Lee Chung-myun.

Korean Times of Utah(2006) H. B. Hulbert and the Song of Arirang. Lee Chung-myun.

Mainichi Shinbun(1927.6.26) The Essence of Folksongs.

Mainichi Shinbun(1934.7.7) The Collection Problem of Folksongs.

Mainichi Shinbun(1960.1.30) Singing the Song of Arirang on the Ship in Snow Drifts Hard day.

Mainichi Shinbun(1990.5.22) The Second see Through the Song of Arirang.

Munhwa Ilbo(2000.8.3) The Story of Japanese Suicide Squad.

Sankei Shinbun(2000.11.28) The Mother of A Suicide Squad: Torihama Dome. Report of Association 'Suicide Squad'.

Segye Ilbo(1958.11.12) Korean Music and its Globalization Problem. Lee Heung-ryeol.

Seoul Shinmun(1956.4.22) Song of Arirang Became the Song of the 7th Division, US Armed Forces in Korea.

Seoul Shinmun(1957.7) The Modernization of Korean Traditional Music.

Seoul Shinmun(1961.4.5) Interchange of Musics between the East and the West, Seoul.

Shinhan Ilbo(1938.9.7) Revolutionalist's Arirang Ballad.

Tongil Shinbo(1983.11.9) For Anti-Japanese Movement of the Ethnical Koreans in Manchuria.

Tongil Shinbo(2002.1.26) A Song of Arirang Engraved in the History of Korea.

■ Lists of Synnara Records

Song of Korea Arirang(1992.7), Synnara Record.

Legends of South and North Korean Arirang(2003.5), Synnara Record.

North Korean Arirang(1999.8), Synnara Record.

Arirang Fantasia 1(2005.3), Synnara Record.

Puzzle of Bonjo Arirang(2005.8), Synnara Record.

Arirang of Korean Peninsula(1994.9), Synnara Record.

Arirang for Overseas Korean(1995.9), Synnara Record.

Arirang in Japan(2002.2), Synnara Record.

Arirang Re-found(2003.2), Synnara Record.

3 Major Jindo Arirang(2003), Synnara Record.

Deagu Arirang(2004.1), Synnara Record.

Jeongseon Arirang(2004), Synnara Record.

Kim Young-im Arirang(2004.11), Synnara Record.

Arirang Nangnang(2005.8), Synnara Record.

Collection of North Korean Arirang(2006.3), Synnara Record.

Arirang Fantasia 2(2006.10), Synnara Record.

Kim San's Arirang(2007.7), Synnara Record.

Arirang, Song of rice(2010), Synnara Record.

Choi Young-sook Arirang(2012), Synnara Record.

Rediscovery of Arirang : Celebration for designation as the UNESCO's
World Heritage.

Arirang of Korea
Han, Sorrows and Hope